Building Wealth: Practical Strategies for Prosperity and Financial Security

Table of Contents

Introduction

- **Purpose of the Book:** Explain the importance of building wealth and financial security.
- **Importance of the Topic:** Discuss why practical strategies are essential for achieving financial prosperity.

Chapter 1: Understanding Wealth

- **Definition of Wealth:** What it means to be wealthy and prosperous.
- **Benefits of Wealth:** How wealth can improve quality of life and provide security.

Chapter 2: Financial Planning

- **Setting Financial Goals:** How to establish short, medium, and long-term financial goals.

- **Budgeting and Expense Control:** Techniques for creating and maintaining an effective budget.

Chapter 3: Debt Management

- **Types of Debt:** The difference between good and bad debt.

- **Debt Repayment Strategies:** Methods like the snowball and avalanche techniques to eliminate debt.

Chapter 4: Savings and Emergency Fund

- **Importance of Savings:** Why having financial reserves is crucial.

- **Building an Emergency Fund:** How much to save and where to keep this money.

Chapter 5: Introduction to Investments

- **Types of Investments:** Stocks, bonds, REITs, cryptocurrencies, and more.

- **Risk and Return:** How to assess the risk and potential return of different investments.

Chapter 6: Portfolio Diversification

- **Importance of Diversification:** How to reduce risks through diversification.
- **Diversification Strategies:** Practical examples of how to diversify an investment portfolio.

Chapter 7: Investments for Beginners

- **First Steps:** How to start investing with little money.
- **Investment Platforms:** Tools and apps that make investing easier for beginners.

Chapter 8: Advanced Investments

- **Fundamental and Technical Analysis:** Methods for evaluating stocks and other assets.
- **Investment Strategies:** Value investing, growth investing, dividend investing, and more.

Chapter 9: Retirement Planning

- **Importance of Retirement Planning:** How to ensure a comfortable retirement.

- **Planning Tools:** Pension plans, long-term investments, and more.

Chapter 10: Financial Education for Families

- **Teaching Finances to Children:** How to introduce financial concepts to the young ones.
- **Family Financial Planning:** How to manage family finances effectively.

Final Chapter: The Beginning of the Practical Journey

Conclusion

- **Summary of Key Points:** Recap of the main lessons from the book.
- **Next Steps:** Guidance on how to continue the journey of building wealth.

Additional Resources

- **Spreadsheets and Tools:** Links to download planning spreadsheets, checklists, and other useful resources.

- **Recommended Reading:** Suggestions for other books and resources to deepen financial knowledge.

Dedication

To my parents, who taught me the value of hard work and perseverance. To my family, whose unconditional support gave me the strength to move forward. To my friends, who always believed in me and encouraged me to reach for my dreams. And to all those who seek to build a secure and prosperous financial future, this book is for you. May it be a source of inspiration and guidance on your journey to prosperity.

Preface

The pursuit of wealth and financial security has fascinated and challenged humanity for centuries. In a constantly changing world where the global economy and personal finances are increasingly interconnected, the need for a deep and practical understanding of how to manage and grow our assets has never been more crucial.

"Building Wealth: Practical Strategies for Prosperity and Financial Security" was born from my own journey and the countless stories I've encountered along the way. Like many of you, I have faced financial challenges, made mistakes, and learned valuable lessons. This book is a culmination of those experiences, combined with extensive research and the wisdom of renowned experts in the field of finance.

Over the years, I have realized that financial education is one of the most powerful tools we can possess. However, it is also one of the most neglected areas in our formal education. Many of us enter adulthood without the necessary skills to manage our finances effectively, which can lead to a range of problems, from overwhelming debt to the inability to plan for the future.

This book was written with the intention of filling that gap. It is designed to be a practical and accessible guide, offering concrete strategies that you can implement immediately to improve your financial situation. Each chapter has been carefully crafted to address different aspects of building wealth, from setting financial goals to diversifying investments and planning for retirement.

One of the key features of this book is its practical approach. It's not just about theory; it's about action. I firmly believe that knowledge is only powerful when applied. Therefore, you will find concrete examples, case studies, and useful tools that will facilitate the application of the discussed concepts. My goal is for you to finish this book not only with a deeper understanding of finances but also with a clear and actionable plan to achieve your financial goals.

Moreover, this book is for everyone. Whether you are a young adult starting your financial journey, an experienced professional looking to optimize your investments, or a parent wanting to teach your children about money, there is something here for you. Building wealth is a continuous process, and regardless of where you are on your journey, there is always room to learn and grow.

I would like to express my gratitude to everyone who contributed to the realization of this book. To the experts who shared their insights, to the friends and family who offered unconditional support, and to you, the reader, for embarking on this journey of financial learning and growth.

I hope that "Building Wealth: Practical Strategies for Prosperity and Financial Security" will be a source of inspiration and guidance for you. May it empower you to make smarter financial decisions, build a secure and prosperous future, and live a full and satisfying life.

With gratitude and enthusiasm, Derik Silva - Author of "Building Wealth: Practical Strategies for Prosperity and Financial Security"

Introduction

Purpose of the Book

Building wealth and achieving financial security are fundamental pillars for a fulfilling and satisfying life. Financial stability not only provides a solid foundation to face daily challenges but also opens doors to new opportunities and experiences that can enrich a person's life in various ways. When you have control over your finances, you can plan for the future with more confidence, invest in personal dreams and projects, and ensure a legacy for future generations.

The importance of building wealth goes beyond simply accumulating money. It's about creating a safety net that allows you to face unforeseen events without compromising your well-being. Financial security offers peace of mind, reduces stress related to monetary issues, and allows people to focus on more meaningful aspects of their lives, such as relationships, health, and personal development.

To achieve this stability, it is essential to have a well-structured financial plan. An effective financial plan helps to set clear goals, organize resources, and make informed decisions. This book is designed to serve as a practical guide, offering strategies and tools that will empower the reader to build wealth gradually and sustainably. Through a practical and action-oriented approach, the reader will learn to manage their finances effectively, eliminate debt, invest wisely, and plan for a secure and independent financial future.

Importance of the Topic

Practical strategies are essential for achieving financial prosperity because they transform theoretical concepts into concrete actions that can be implemented in daily life. Financial theory, no matter how robust and well-founded, only becomes truly valuable when applied practically. It is through practical application that people can see tangible and measurable results in their personal finances.

For example, understanding the concept of compound interest is important, but knowing how to apply it in real investments is what truly makes a difference. Similarly, knowing the importance of an emergency fund is useful, but creating and maintaining that fund is what provides financial security. Practical strategies help transform knowledge into action, allowing people to make smarter and more effective financial decisions.

To illustrate the importance of a practical approach, we can consider examples of success and failure. Think of a person who understands the theory behind investment diversification but does not apply it. This person might end up investing all their money in a single asset, taking unnecessary risks. On the other hand, someone who practically applies the theory of diversification, spreading their investments across different asset classes, will be better protected against market volatility and have a greater chance of achieving their financial goals.

Another example is debt management. Knowing that it is important to pay off debt is one thing, but applying practical strategies like the snowball or avalanche method can significantly accelerate the debt repayment process, providing faster financial relief.

This book aims to provide these practical strategies, based on solid financial principles but always with a focus on real-world application. Through concrete examples, case studies, and useful tools, the reader will be empowered to take control of their finances and make conscious decisions to achieve their goals. The practical and action-oriented approach of this book will ensure that the knowledge gained is transformed into real and lasting results.

Chapter 1: Understanding Wealth

Definition of Wealth

The definition of wealth can vary widely depending on who is defining it and the context in which it is discussed. Traditionally, wealth is associated with the possession of substantial material goods and financial resources. However, this view is just one facet of a much broader and multifaceted concept.

Financial Aspects: In the most direct sense, being wealthy means having a significant amount of financial assets, such as money, properties, investments, and other valuable items. Financial wealth allows for the acquisition of goods and services, the ability to make investments, and the capacity to handle emergencies without compromising one's standard of living. However, financial wealth is not an end in itself but a means to achieve other goals and provide security and comfort.

Emotional Aspects: Emotional wealth refers to psychological well-being and personal satisfaction. A person may have limited financial resources but still feel wealthy due to healthy relationships, a balanced life, and the ability to find joy in small things. Emotional wealth is often underestimated but is crucial for a fulfilling and satisfying life. It includes aspects such as happiness, peace of mind, self-esteem, and the ability to cope with emotional challenges.

Social Aspects: Social wealth involves the quality and quantity of interpersonal relationships and support networks. Having a strong network of friends, family, and colleagues can be an invaluable source of emotional and practical support. Social wealth also includes respect and reputation within a community, as well as the ability to influence and contribute positively to society.

Cultural Perspectives: The perception of wealth can vary significantly across different cultures. In some societies, wealth is primarily measured in financial and material terms, while in others, aspects such as family harmony, health, and community contribution may be considered equally or more important. For example, in collectivist cultures, wealth may be seen in terms of collective well-being and mutual support, whereas in individualist cultures, the emphasis may be more on personal achievement and the accumulation of individual assets.

Individual Variations: Even within the same culture, the perception of wealth can vary from person to person. For some, being wealthy might mean having the financial freedom to travel and explore the world, while for others, it might mean owning a home and providing stability for their family. The definition of wealth is, therefore, highly subjective and can be influenced by personal values, life experiences, and aspirations.

Benefits of Wealth

Wealth, in its various forms, can bring a range of benefits that improve quality of life and provide security. These benefits can be tangible, such as the ability to acquire goods and services, and intangible, such as reduced stress and improved overall well-being.

Tangible Benefits:

1. **Acquisition Capability:** Financial wealth allows for the acquisition of goods and services that can significantly improve quality of life. This includes basic necessities like food and housing, as well as luxuries like travel and entertainment. The ability to acquire quality goods can provide comfort and convenience, contributing to a more enjoyable lifestyle.

2. **Investments and Growth:** With sufficient financial resources, it is possible to make investments that can generate returns and further increase wealth. Investing in stocks, real estate, businesses, and other opportunities can provide an additional source of income and help build a solid financial foundation over time.

3. **Education and Development:** Wealth enables access to quality education, which is a cornerstone for personal and professional development. Investing in education, whether for oneself or for one's children, can open doors to better career opportunities and personal growth.

4. **Health and Well-being:** Having sufficient financial resources allows access to quality healthcare, including medical treatments, health insurance, and wellness programs. The ability to take care of physical and mental health is fundamental for a long and healthy life.

Intangible Benefits:

1. **Stress Reduction:** Financial security significantly reduces stress related to monetary issues. Knowing that there are sufficient resources to handle emergencies and unforeseen events provides a sense of security and tranquility. This, in turn, can improve mental and emotional health.

2. **Freedom and Flexibility:** Wealth offers the freedom to make choices that might otherwise be impossible. This includes the ability to change careers, travel, dedicate time to hobbies and personal interests, and even retire early. The flexibility provided by wealth allows people to live according to their own terms and values.

3. **Contribution and Legacy:** Wealth also enables people to contribute to causes and communities that are important to them. Donations to charity, investments in community projects, and creating a legacy for future generations are ways to use wealth to make a positive difference in the world.

4. **Self-esteem and Fulfillment:** The ability to achieve financial goals and build wealth can increase self-esteem and a sense of personal fulfillment. Feeling financially secure and successful can provide a sense of pride and satisfaction, contributing to overall well-being.

Case Studies:

1. **Success Story:** Consider the example of Maria, an IT professional who started investing in stocks and real estate at the age of 30. With a well-planned strategy and financial discipline, Maria managed to build a diversified portfolio that provided her with substantial passive income. By the age of 45, she decided to reduce her workload to focus on personal projects and

travel. The financial security Maria built allowed her to live according to her values and interests without compromising her standard of living.

2. **Failure Story:** On the other hand, we have the example of John, who inherited a large sum of money but lacked the financial knowledge to manage it properly. John spent most of the money on luxury items and high-risk investments without proper research. Within a few years, he lost most of his wealth and faced financial difficulties. This example illustrates the importance of practical strategies and financial knowledge to maintain and grow wealth.

Prepare Your Mind

In this first chapter of the book, we start with the principle that all knowledge needs to be built on a solid foundation. Therefore, regardless of what phase you are in—whether you are an experienced investor or someone with no knowledge of investments—it is important to start with the basics to reach the pinnacle: becoming a complete investor. Thus, before learning about Fixed Income, Variable Income, Market Markings, and other investment skills, it is necessary to incorporate some information into your mindset that will help you learn better, visualize your strategies, and value each piece of content presented to you.

Building Wealth: This preparation will help you understand that getting rich, besides not being just a monetary issue, is not something that happens overnight. It is not something easy or effortless; it requires mental preparation to view your financial life differently.

Much is said about what money cannot buy. Here, we will talk about what money CAN buy. We will discuss money and the power it provides us.

A large portion of Americans is financially illiterate. This means that they are people who know nothing about wealth management, the potential to increase their income, and improve their quality of life. It is very rare, even among highly educated professionals, for them to know how to invest their own money. Even if they speak many languages, the language of money and capitalism is the one that truly matters in today's world. It is essential to master it. Mainly, to free oneself from the slavery that this logic of money imposes on everyone. And basically, only money itself can remove the economic shackles. Your money's initial purpose should be to provide you with freedom.

In a vicious cycle where consumption is an imperative that forces people to seek to own things, in the end, it is the things that own them. This is the phrase we take from the movie "Fight Club" that perfectly defines reality: "We work jobs we hate to buy things we don't need."

The goal of the book "Building Wealth" is precisely to offer technical knowledge while giving you the chance to see the entire financial landscape around us and how we can use it to our advantage.

"The poor work for money, and the rich make money work for them."

Why Do the Rich Get Richer?

You may have wondered why the rich get richer and the poor get poorer. The explanation for this begins with one of the most famous cynics in history: Diogenes. And do not think that the meaning of cynicism here is the same as we know today, of someone sarcastic or mocking. The primary meaning of this word comes from periods before Christ when cynicism was a Greek philosophical movement that preached simplicity, rejecting wealth and ostentation. The cynics lived in search of beings with honesty.

The very figure of Diogenes is present in various stories that represent how he and his peers lived the beliefs they held. There is a famous image of the visit of King Alexander the Great to the place where Diogenes lived: a barrel. The monarch asked the man there, what he, as a king full of wealth and power, could do for him. The man replied that he would just like Alexander to move away from the sun because he was blocking the sunlight, which at that moment was all he really needed. Despite figures like Alexander being famous for their fragile egos and cruelty towards those who disagreed, what happened was unexpected. Alexander felt admiration for Diogenes' security and conviction, requiring only something basic that did not depend on what the high echelon could provide. Alexander, according to the books, even said that if he could choose, he would like to be Diogenes himself.

This is because, for the cynics, it was worth giving up luxuries and pleasures to have full freedom, something that, in their view, was impossible to achieve while being attached to something. Despite this, the view of the Greek cynics is not absolute and can easily be reflected upon and contrasted with other philosophies. But the essential part of them, for our purpose, is to ask these questions. What do you really need to live? Why do you need them? Do you have a job that binds you because of debts you incurred that do not necessarily represent you? Are your debts things you truly enjoy, or do they serve as a display for people and interest groups? After reflecting on this, get rid of what you do not need to live and enjoy life well. Keep only your pleasures and items that have value in your own conception.

Moving on to the explanation of why the rich get richer and the poor get poorer, we can be very direct. The poor buy liabilities. The rich buy assets. A liability is anything that does not provide you with any value but costs you. An asset, on the other hand, is something that, even if it has costs, generates income. A car, for example, is almost always a liability. Unless, of course, you rent it out or use it in a ride-sharing app that will earn you money. In summary, what puts money in your pocket is an ASSET. What takes it out is a liability.

Obviously, it is very unlikely to live without any liabilities, so it is very important to ensure that liabilities are worth the cost. Many poor people end up sinking deeper and deeper, trying to mimic the acquisitions of the rich without thinking that they have not expanded their asset column. All the money in the world, if not converted into ASSETS, can disappear. And the opposite is also true. Once you have a good column of ASSETS, it is possible to bounce back even after dealing with market setbacks (in the digital module, you can download the spreadsheet and fill in your assets and liabilities to find out if you are on the right track).

To conclude, two phrases to memorize:

- "The poor work for money, and the rich make money work for them." - Robert Kiyosaki
- "If you are born poor, it is not your fault. But if you die poor, it is your fault." - Bill Gates

Limiting Beliefs

One very important thing is to observe what are the first phrases that come to your mind when you think about money. This is because, in society, many ideas about money have been disseminated, and they can prevent you from seeing money with the importance it deserves. First of all, there is no chance of accumulating money while you have anger towards it. If you doubt this, it is likely to harm you because it is not logic that governs the world. In the world, especially in the financial market, opinions do not have the same value as facts, as they do not change based on beliefs.

If the phrases you list in your mind about money are mostly positive, that is a good sign, as your mindset will tend to favor wealth accumulation. The exact opposite occurs when you have very negative views about money, as these views become limiting beliefs that can end up being obstacles, especially mental ones, and if this is the case, you need to readjust your mindset. Do not blame yourself for this. It is possible that negative beliefs come from financial problems experienced since childhood, religious or ideological influences, and even unsuccessful experiences that have been part of your journey. However, it is urgent to make this adjustment to achieve the goal of having money, and for that, you need to like it and see it as something essential.

Some of the most common myths include 'money is the root of all evil,' when, in fact, problems related to money come from the lack of it. If money were bad, it would be distributed and not pursued. Another myth is that money is linked to luck. The reality is that it is necessary to be in the right place, at the right time, and be the right person for a particular situation. In summary, having a favorable situation and an appropriate moment is not a guarantee of the so-called assertive reward. It is like saying that buying supplements and just being inside a gym will make you a muscular individual. It is essential that, in addition to going to the gym, using the supplements correctly, the individual exercises with discipline, has a rigorous diet based on their purpose, and takes advantage of the time and place to put in their effort (which will make them the right person, in the right place, at the right time for this purpose).

Excellent opportunities given to different people produce different results precisely because luck is not in the opportunity. Success is tied to the use each person makes of the scenario they are placed in.

There is also the myth that the rich are selfish. The reality is that the amount of money an individual earns is related to the number of people that person impacts with their actions. And, indeed, just observe the news that many billionaires make a difference in the lives of many people, improving their lives. Many of them even engage in philanthropy, which further increases the positive impact on others' lives. No one gets rich without creating some impact on many people's lives. Money is always a RESULT.

There is also the erroneous maxim that 'money does not bring happiness.' Nothing could be more wrong than this view because money buys the only thing worth having in life: FREEDOM. From freedom, all things can be, or not, acquired, can be done or not. This, along with health and human relationships, makes up the basic triad for world fulfillment.

There is also the idea, also incorrect, that money turns people into bad people. The truth is that money only intensifies what already exists in someone. If a person is necessarily bad, they will become even worse. The same applies to good people who, even before having money, are naturally generous; when they accumulate money, they will do even more good things, help others, and so on.

They also say that money is dirty. In the literal sense, it is true. Cash is not very hygienic. Credit cards, in this case, would be more appropriate. But jokes aside, money is the result of merit. Moreover, they say that the amount of money in the world is limited. In this case, just look at history to recognize that the amount of money has increased exponentially over time. Wealth can be created, industrial and agricultural production expands, and the creation of money issued by governments also follows the economy. A valuable detail is that, when evaluating the historical trajectory, the global panorama regarding poverty has improved significantly, although it remains in very high numbers.

Finally, there is still the belief that the rich get rich at the expense of the poor. Another inconsistency. To begin with, it is impossible to find a single billionaire who has not produced millionaires along the way.

Moreover, people with money need others with the financial means to consume the products or services they sell. This idea was invented to curb voluntary exchanges. Is there exploitation in the world? Yes! But that has nothing to do with capital accumulation.

It is also not uncommon to hear that it is unfair to think about having X when there are millions of people starving. This view is a fallacy because it gives the false idea that not having money will reduce the number of poor people in the world. And the stark reality is that not having money will only increase one more poor person, while being rich can reduce one or more. The guilt created in becoming rich does not solve the problem; it only perpetuates a reality you disapprove of.

To conclude, two final myths. The first: if someone got rich, it is because they stole. First of all, how many thieves do you know outside of white-collar criminals? The reality is that a thief has money sporadically and not consistently. And finally, the second: 'only those who have money make money.' This second myth is proven false because, in the information age, it is possible to create money with practically nothing, which means it is possible to invest little and profit significantly more.

Of course, there are other falsehoods out there that try to tarnish the reputation of money and sabotage the pursuit of it. And these notions need to be eliminated because, truly, only those who like money make money.

Conclusion: Wealth can improve quality of life in various ways, providing both tangible and intangible benefits. The ability to acquire goods and services, invest in growth, access education, and healthcare are just some of the tangible benefits. Stress reduction, freedom, contribution to society, and increased self-esteem are intangible benefits that are also extremely valuable. Understanding and valuing these benefits can motivate people to pursue wealth-building in a conscious and strategic manner.

Chapter 2: Financial Planning

Before anything else, the first step is to distinguish what money can and cannot buy. It is crucial to understand that the most valuable thing money can provide is your FREEDOM. For example, if you stopped working today, what would happen to your life from that moment on? Most likely, you wouldn't be able to pay your bills (like mortgages, car payments, taxes, etc.), you wouldn't be able to leave your house, and you certainly couldn't buy anything that brings you pleasure. You would be at real risk of becoming homeless in a short period. This happens simply because you never planned or cared about your financial future.

In this book, we will learn how to achieve 'Financial Freedom.' How to own more assets than liabilities without having to work more to make it happen.

First, we need to free ourselves from the chains we've created throughout our lives. Pay off debts we shouldn't have incurred, whether it's the car bought prematurely or the apartment acquired hastily. And once we learn more about investments, we will be the masters of our own destiny, meaning we can achieve FREEDOM, which is the only asset we should aspire to in life.

Setting Financial Goals

Establishing financial goals is a crucial step toward achieving prosperity and financial security. Well-defined goals serve as a roadmap, guiding your financial decisions and actions. They help maintain the focus, motivation, and discipline needed to reach your objectives. Let's explore how to set short, medium, and long-term financial goals, the importance of having clear and measurable objectives, and practical examples of financial goals.

Short-Term Goals: Short-term goals are those you aim to achieve within a year. They are essential for creating a solid financial foundation and can include objectives such as:

Creating an Emergency Fund:

- **Objective:** Accumulate an emergency fund equivalent to three to six months of expenses.

- **Importance:** An emergency fund provides a safety net for unforeseen events, such as job loss or unexpected medical expenses.

- **How to Achieve:** Set a specific amount based on your monthly expenses. Automate monthly transfers to a dedicated savings account until you reach your goal.

2. **Paying Off Credit Card Debt:**

    - **Objective:** Eliminate the outstanding balance on your credit card.

    - **Importance:** Credit card debt typically has high-interest rates, which can hinder financial progress.

    - **How to Achieve:** Use strategies like the snowball method (paying off the smallest debts first) or the avalanche method (paying off the highest interest debts first). Reduce unnecessary expenses and direct those funds toward debt repayment.

3. **Saving for a Specific Purchase:**

    - **Objective:** Save for a planned purchase, such as a trip or a new appliance.

    - **Importance:** Planning and saving for purchases avoids the use of credit and unnecessary debt.

    - **How to Achieve:** Estimate the cost of the purchase and divide it by the number of months until the desired date. Automate monthly transfers to a specific savings account.

Medium-Term Goals: Medium-term goals are those you aim to achieve within one to five years. They generally involve larger objectives that require continuous planning and discipline. Examples include:

1. **Buying a Car:**

    - **Objective:** Save for a down payment or to buy a car outright.

- **Importance:** Buying a car outright or with a substantial down payment can reduce or eliminate the need for financing, saving on interest.

- **How to Achieve:** Research the cost of the desired car and estimate the down payment or full payment amount. Create a monthly savings plan and adjust your budget to accommodate this goal.

2. **Paying Off Student Loans:**

    - **Objective:** Pay off student loans.

    - **Importance:** Eliminating student debt can free up resources for other financial goals and reduce financial stress.

    - **How to Achieve:** Make extra payments whenever possible and consider refinancing for better interest rates. Direct bonuses or salary increases toward debt repayment.

3. **Saving for a Home Down Payment:**

- **Objective:** Accumulate a substantial down payment for purchasing a home.
- **Importance:** A larger down payment can reduce the amount of financing needed and lower interest rates.
- **How to Achieve:** Determine the down payment amount based on the price of the desired home. Automate monthly transfers to a dedicated savings account and consider low-risk investments to increase the accumulated amount.

Long-Term Goals: Long-term goals are those you aim to achieve over a period longer than five years. They generally involve significant life objectives and require continuous planning and investment. Examples include:

1. **Comfortable Retirement:**
    - **Objective:** Accumulate enough wealth to ensure a comfortable retirement.
    - **Importance:** Planning for retirement is essential to ensure financial security in old age.

- **How to Achieve:** Regularly contribute to private pension plans and retirement accounts. Diversify your investments and adjust your contributions as needed to reach the desired amount.

2. **Children's Education:**

    - **Objective:** Save for your children's college education.
    - **Importance:** Ensuring resources for your children's education can provide better career opportunities and personal growth.
    - **How to Achieve:** Estimate the education costs and create a monthly savings plan. Consider educational savings accounts and long-term investments to maximize capital growth.

3. **Real Estate Investment:**

    - **Objective:** Acquire properties for investment or personal use.

- **Importance:** Investing in real estate can generate passive income and increase wealth.

- **How to Achieve:** Research the real estate market and determine the necessary amount for the purchase. Create a savings and investment plan to accumulate the required amount.

Importance of Clear and Measurable Goals: Having clear and measurable objectives is fundamental to financial success. Well-defined goals help maintain focus and motivation, as well as provide criteria for measuring progress. To set effective goals, use the SMART method (Specific, Measurable, Achievable, Relevant, Time-bound):

- **Specific:** Define clear and detailed goals.

- **Measurable:** Establish criteria to measure progress.

- **Achievable:** Ensure the goal is realistic.

- **Relevant:** Make sure the goal is important to you.

- **Time-bound:** Set a deadline to achieve the goal.

Examples of Financial Goals:

1. **Short-Term:** Save $5,000 in six months for an emergency fund.//
2. **Medium-Term:** Pay off $20,000 in student loans in three years.
3. **Long-Term:** Accumulate $1,000,000 for retirement in 30 years.

Conclusion: Setting short, medium, and long-term financial goals is essential for achieving financial prosperity. Clear and measurable goals help maintain focus and motivation, as well as provide criteria for measuring progress. With a well-structured plan and discipline, it is possible to achieve your financial objectives and ensure a secure and prosperous future.

Budgeting and Expense Control

Creating and maintaining an effective budget is one of the most important financial skills you can develop. A well-crafted budget helps control spending, save money, and achieve your financial goals. Let's explore techniques for creating and maintaining an effective budget, the importance of expense control, and practical tools to help in this process.

Importance of Expense Control: Expense control is fundamental to financial health. Without proper control, it is easy to spend more than you earn, accumulating debt and compromising your ability to save and invest. An effective budget helps identify areas where expenses can be reduced and directs resources to priority financial goals.

Steps to Create an Effective Budget:

1. **Assess Your Current Financial Situation:**

    - **Income:** List all sources of income, including salary, bonuses, investment returns, and other sources.

    - **Expenses:** Categorize your expenses into fixed (rent, mortgage, utilities) and variable (food, entertainment, travel).

2. **Set Financial Goals:**

- Establish short, medium, and long-term goals as discussed earlier. These goals will guide your budgeting and expense control decisions.

3. **Create Expense Categories:**

    - Divide your expenses into categories such as housing, transportation, food, health, leisure, and savings. This will help visualize where your money is being spent and identify areas for adjustments.

4. **Assign Values to Categories:**

    - Based on your income and financial goals, assign specific amounts to each expense category. Ensure that your total expenses do not exceed your income.

5. **Monitor and Adjust:**

    - Regularly track your expenses and compare them with the planned budget. Make adjustments as necessary to ensure you are on track to achieve your goals.

Tools and Practical Methods:

1. **Budget Spreadsheets:**

    - **Excel or Google Sheets:** Create a personalized spreadsheet to track your income and expenses. Use formulas to automatically calculate totals and differences.

    - **Pre-made Templates:** Use online budget templates that come with pre-configured categories and formulas.

2. **Budgeting Apps:**

    - **Mint:** A free app that connects your bank accounts and credit cards, automatically categorizing your transactions and providing detailed reports.

    - **YNAB (You Need A Budget):** A paid app that helps create a goal-based budget and track your expenses in real-time.

    - **PocketGuard:** An app that shows how much money you have available to spend after considering your savings goals and fixed expenses.

3. **Envelope Method:**
   - **Physical:** Separate money into physical envelopes for each expense category. When the money in an envelope runs out, you cannot spend more in that category until the next period.
   - **Digital:** Use apps like Goodbudget to create digital envelopes and track your expenses similarly.

4. **50/30/20 Method:**
   - **50% Needs:** Allocate 50% of your income to essential needs such as housing, food, and transportation.
   - **30% Wants:** Reserve 30% for wants and leisure, such as entertainment and travel.
   - **20% Savings and Debt:** Direct 20% to savings and debt repayment.

Tips for Maintaining an Effective Budget:

1. **Review Regularly:**

- Review your budget monthly to ensure it still reflects your financial situation and goals. Make adjustments as necessary.

2. **Be Realistic:**

    - Be honest about your spending habits and adjust your budget to reflect reality. Unrealistic goals can lead to frustration and abandonment of the budget.

3. **Automate Savings:**

    - Set up automatic transfers to savings and investment accounts. This ensures you save regularly without having to think about it.

4. **Reduce Unnecessary Expenses:**

    - Identify areas where you can cut unnecessary spending. Small savings can add up over time and free up resources for more important goals.

5. **Use Rewards:**

- Reward yourself for achieving financial goals. Small rewards can keep you motivated and make the budgeting process more enjoyable.

Practical Examples:

1. **Example of a Monthly Budget:**
    - **Income:** $5,000
    - **Fixed Expenses:**
        - Rent: $1,500
        - Utilities: $300
        - Transportation: $400
    - **Variable Expenses:**
        - Food: $800
        - Leisure: $500
        - Health: $200
    - **Savings and Investments:**
        - Emergency Fund: $500
        - Investments: $300

- **Total Expenses:** $4,500
- **Remaining Balance:** $500 (can be directed to additional goals or savings)

2. **Example of Budget Adjustment:**
   - **Situation:** John realizes he is spending $200 more on food than planned.
   - **Action:** He decides to reduce leisure spending by $100 and adjust his grocery shopping to save the other $100. He also starts cooking more at home to reduce restaurant expenses.

Conclusion: Creating and maintaining an effective budget is essential for achieving your financial goals and ensuring long-term financial health. Expense control helps avoid unnecessary debt and directs resources to important priorities. With the use of practical tools like spreadsheets and budgeting apps, and the application of proven methods like the envelope method and the 50/30/20 method, it is possible to develop a budget that works for you. Discipline and regular review are key to keeping the budget on track and achieving financial prosperity.

Chapter 3: Debt Management

When it comes to financial organization, the first crucial step is identifying where your money is going. What are you spending on? Where is it being drained? With the advancement of technology, there are tools that can greatly facilitate this process. One example is the app Mint, which helps connect your expenses and organize your finances more efficiently. This app is especially useful for those who use credit cards, debit cards, or make bank transfers, as it can automatically sync these transactions.

For those who prefer to use cash, the process can be a bit more labor-intensive, as it will require manually recording each expense. However, this practice of manual recording can be an excellent way to increase awareness of your spending habits. It is highly recommended to avoid cash withdrawals whenever possible, as cash tends to be spent more quickly and is harder to track. The saying "money in hand is like sand in the wind" aptly illustrates this situation, highlighting how easily physical money can disappear without clear traces of where it was spent.

Debt management is an essential skill for achieving financial stability and, eventually, financial freedom. Understanding the different types of debt and effective strategies for paying them off can transform how you handle your finances, allowing you to break free from the burden of financial obligations and start building wealth sustainably.

Types of Debt

Debts can be classified into two main categories: good debt and bad debt. Understanding the difference between them is crucial for managing your finances effectively.

Good Debt

Good debt is debt that has the potential to increase your net worth or improve your financial situation over the long term. They are generally associated with investments that generate returns or provide significant benefits. Here are some examples of good debt:

1. **Mortgages:** A mortgage is a loan used to buy a home. Although it is a significant debt, it is considered good debt because the property

tends to appreciate over time. Additionally, owning a home can provide stability and financial security. In many cases, the interest paid on a mortgage can be deducted from taxes, which can reduce the overall cost of the loan.

2. **Student Loans:** Investing in education can significantly increase your earning potential over your lifetime. A college degree or professional qualification can open doors to better job opportunities and higher salaries. Although student loans can be a financial burden, they are considered good debt because the return on investment in education is generally high.

3. **Business Loans:** Taking out a loan to start or expand a business can be good debt if the business has the potential to generate profit. A successful business can provide a significant source of income and increase your net worth. However, it is important to conduct careful analysis and have a solid business plan before taking on this type of debt.

Bad Debt

Bad debt is debt that does not generate returns and can harm your financial health. They generally have high-interest rates and are used to finance consumer goods that depreciate in value. Here are some examples of bad debt:

1. **High-Interest Credit Cards:** Credit card debt is one of the most common forms of bad debt. Credit card interest rates can be extremely high, making it difficult to pay off the balance in full. Additionally, items purchased with credit cards generally depreciate in value, meaning you are paying interest on something that is no longer worth what you paid for it.

2. **Personal Loans for Consumption:** Personal loans used to finance consumer purchases, such as electronics, clothing, or vacations, are considered bad debt. These items do not generate financial returns and generally lose value quickly. Paying interest on these purchases can hinder your ability to save and invest.

3. **Car Financing:** Although a car may be a necessity, financing it can be bad debt if you

cannot pay the full amount quickly. Cars depreciate in value as soon as they leave the dealership, and paying interest on an asset that is losing value can be financially detrimental.

4. **Consortiums: A Disguised Bad Debt?** Consortiums are often presented as a viable alternative to traditional financing, especially for those who want to acquire property without paying interest. However, it is crucial to understand that consortiums also have financial pitfalls that can make them a less attractive option than they initially seem.

Administration Fees and INCC

Although consortiums do not charge interest, they include an administration fee that can be quite significant. Additionally, consortiums are subject to the National Construction Cost Index (INCC), which measures the variation in the costs of inputs used in residential construction. This index, calculated by the Getúlio Vargas Foundation (FGV), can cause the total amount paid for the consortium to be higher than initially anticipated.

How Consortiums Work

A consortium brings together a group of people interested in acquiring property, who commit to paying a fixed monthly amount. The consortium administrator conducts periodic draws to determine who will receive the credit letter, which can be used to purchase the property. Until you are selected, you continue to pay the consortium installments, in addition to the administration fees that ensure the maintenance of the managing company and cover any defaults.

Hidden Costs and Adjustments

Initially, the total amount of the consortium may seem attractive, as it is presented as a fixed amount. However, this amount is often adjusted based on the INCC, which can result in significant additional costs over time. Additionally, while waiting to be selected, you may need to pay rent or other housing expenses, which further increases the total cost.

Comparison with Financing

Although traditional financing also has its disadvantages, such as high-interest rates, it offers more predictability in terms of costs. Financing installments are generally fixed or adjusted according to more stable parameters, which can facilitate long-term financial planning.

Impact on Financial Health

How you manage your debts can have a significant impact on your financial health. Good debt, when managed correctly, can help build wealth and improve your financial situation over the long term. However, bad debt can quickly become a financial burden, making it difficult to save, invest, and achieve your financial goals.

For example, if you have a large amount of high-interest credit card debt, a significant portion of your monthly income may be allocated to paying interest, leaving less money available for other needs and financial goals. This can create a vicious cycle of indebtedness, where you are constantly struggling to pay off your debts without making significant progress.

On the other hand, if you have a mortgage or student loan, these payments can be seen as investments in your future. While it is still important to manage these debts responsibly, they have the potential to provide long-term financial benefits.

Debt Repayment Strategies

There are several effective strategies for eliminating debt, and two of the most popular are the snowball and avalanche methods. Each strategy has its own advantages and disadvantages, and the best approach depends on your financial situation and personal preferences.

Snowball Method

The snowball method is a psychological approach to debt repayment that focuses on paying off the smallest debts first. Here's how it works:

1. **List Your Debts:** Make a list of all your debts, ranking them from smallest to largest, regardless of the interest rate.

2. **Pay the Smallest Debt First:** Focus on paying off the smallest debt first while making minimum payments on all other debts. Put all extra money you can towards the smallest debt until it is fully paid off.

3. **Move to the Next Debt:** After paying off the smallest debt, move to the next debt on the list. Use the money you were paying on the previous debt to help pay off the next debt, creating a snowball effect.

4. **Repeat the Process:** Continue this process until all your debts are paid off.

Advantages of the Snowball Method

- **Motivation:** Paying off smaller debts quickly can provide a sense of accomplishment and motivation to continue the process. Each paid-off debt is a victory that can boost your confidence and determination.

- **Simplicity:** The snowball method is simple and easy to follow. It doesn't require complex interest calculations, just a list of debts and a plan to pay them off.

Disadvantages of the Snowball Method

- **Total Cost:** The snowball method can result in a higher total cost in interest, especially if you have larger debts with high-interest rates.

Focusing on smaller debts first may mean you are paying more interest over time.

Practical Example of the Snowball Method

Let's consider a practical example to illustrate the snowball method. Suppose you have the following debts:

- **Credit Card A:** $500 with 18% interest
- **Personal Loan:** $1,500 with 12% interest
- **Credit Card B:** $2,000 with 20% interest
- **Student Loan:** $5,000 with 6% interest

Using the snowball method, you would start by paying off Credit Card A first. Suppose you can pay $200 per month. You would make minimum payments on all other debts and put the remaining money towards Credit Card A until it is paid off. After paying off Credit Card A, you would move to the Personal Loan, using the $200 plus the minimum payment you were making on Credit Card A. This process would continue until all debts are paid off.

Avalanche Method

The avalanche method is a mathematical approach to debt repayment that focuses on paying off the debts with the highest interest rates first. Here's how it works:

1. **List Your Debts:** Make a list of all your debts, ranking them from highest to lowest interest rate.

2. **Pay the Highest Interest Debt First:** Focus on paying off the debt with the highest interest rate first while making minimum payments on all other debts. Put all extra money you can towards the highest interest debt until it is fully paid off.

3. **Move to the Next Debt:** After paying off the highest interest debt, move to the next debt on the list. Use the money you were paying on the previous debt to help pay off the next debt.

4. **Repeat the Process:** Continue this process until all your debts are paid off.

Advantages of the Avalanche Method

- **Interest Savings:** The avalanche method can result in significant interest savings over time, as you are focusing on the most expensive debts first.

- **Total Cost Reduction:** By paying off the debts with the highest interest rates first, you can reduce the total cost of your debts more quickly.

Disadvantages of the Avalanche Method

- **Motivation:** The avalanche method can be less motivating than the snowball method, especially if the debts with the highest interest rates are also the largest in value. It may take longer to see significant progress, which can be demotivating for some people.

- **Complexity:** The avalanche method can be more complex to follow, as it requires interest calculations and a more detailed analysis of your debts.

Practical Example of the Avalanche Method

Let's consider the same practical example to illustrate the avalanche method. Suppose you have the following debts:

- **Credit Card A:** $500 with 18% interest
- **Personal Loan:** $1,500 with 12% interest
- **Credit Card B:** $2,000 with 20% interest
- **Student Loan:** $5,000 with 6% interest

Using the avalanche method, you would start by paying off Credit Card B first, as it has the highest interest rate. Suppose you can pay $200 per month. You would make minimum payments on all other debts and put the remaining money towards Credit Card B until it is paid off. After paying off Credit Card B, you would move to Credit Card A, using the $200 plus the minimum payment you were making on Credit Card B. This process would continue until all debts are paid off.

Comparison Between Methods

Both the snowball and avalanche methods have their own advantages and disadvantages, and the best approach depends on your financial situation and personal preferences. Here is a comparison between the two methods:

CRITERION	SNOWBALL METHOD	AVALANCHE METHOD
Initial Focus	Smaller debts	Debts with highest interest
Motivation	High (quick wins)	Moderate (slower wins)
Interest Savings	Lower	Higher
Complexity	Low	High
Total Cost	Higher	Lower

Choosing the Best Strategy

The choice between the snowball method and the avalanche method depends on your priorities and personal preferences. If you need motivation and like to see quick progress, the snowball method may be the best option for you. However, if you are focused on saving as much as possible on interest and are willing to follow a more mathematical approach, the avalanche method may be more suitable.

Regardless of the method you choose, the most important thing is to have a plan and follow it consistently. Debt repayment requires discipline, patience, and commitment, but the benefits of becoming debt-free and achieving financial freedom are well worth the effort.

Case Studies

Let's consider some case studies to illustrate the application of the snowball and avalanche methods.

Case Study 1: Snowball Method

Maria has the following debts:

- **Credit Card A:** $300 with 15% interest
- **Personal Loan:** $1,200 with 10% interest
- **Credit Card B:** $2,500 with 18% interest
- **Student Loan:** $4,000 with 5% interest

Maria decides to use the snowball method to pay off her debts. She makes a list of her debts from smallest to largest and starts by paying off Credit Card A first. She can pay $250 per month. Here is Maria's plan:

1. **Credit Card A:** Maria pays $250 per month until the $300 balance is paid off in two months.

2. **Personal Loan:** After paying off Credit Card A, Maria uses the $250 plus the minimum payment she was making on Credit Card A to pay off the Personal Loan. She pays $300 per month until the $1,200 balance is paid off in four months.

3. **Credit Card B:** After paying off the Personal Loan, Maria uses the $300 plus the minimum payment she was making on the Personal Loan to pay off Credit Card B. She pays $350 per month until the $2,500 balance is paid off in seven months.

4. **Student Loan:** Finally, Maria uses the $350 plus the minimum payment she was making on Credit Card B to pay off the Student Loan. She pays $400 per month until the $4,000 balance is paid off in ten months.

Maria manages to pay off all her debts in a total of 23 months, feeling motivated and accomplished with each debt paid off.

Case Study 2: Avalanche Method

John has the following debts:

- **Credit Card A:** $500 with 20% interest
- **Personal Loan:** $1,500 with 12% interest
- **Credit Card B:** $2,000 with 18% interest
- **Student Loan:** $5,000 with 6% interest

John decides to use the avalanche method to pay off his debts. He makes a list of his debts from highest to lowest interest rate and starts by paying off Credit Card A first. He can pay $300 per month. Here is John's plan:

1. **Credit Card A:** John pays $300 per month until the $500 balance is paid off in two months.

2. **Credit Card B:** After paying off Credit Card A, John uses the $300 plus the minimum payment he was making on Credit Card A to pay off Credit Card B. He pays $350 per month until the $2,000 balance is paid off in six months.

3. **Personal Loan:** After paying off Credit Card B, John uses the $350 plus the minimum payment he was making on Credit Card B to pay off the Personal Loan. He pays $400 per month until the $1,500 balance is paid off in four months.

4. **Student Loan:** Finally, John uses the $400 plus the minimum payment he was making on the Personal Loan to pay off the Student Loan. He pays $450 per month until the $5,000 balance is paid off in eleven months.

John manages to pay off all his debts in a total of 23 months, saving more on interest over time.

Conclusion

Debt management is a crucial part of building wealth and financial security. Understanding the difference between good and bad debt and applying effective debt repayment strategies can transform your financial situation and help you achieve your goals. Whether using the snowball method or the avalanche method, the most important thing is to have a plan, follow it consistently, and stay motivated along the way. Financial freedom is achievable, and with the right tools and strategies, you can break free from debt and start building a prosperous and secure financial future.

Chapter 4: Savings and Emergency Fund

Importance of Savings

The importance of having a financial reserve cannot be overstated. Savings are the foundation of a healthy and stable financial life, providing a safety net that can be crucial in times of uncertainty. Regular saving is a habit that can transform the way you handle your finances, offering a range of benefits from peace of mind to the ability to seize financial opportunities.

Benefits of Regular Saving

1. **Financial Security in Uncertain Times:** Life is full of unexpected events. Unforeseen medical expenses, job loss, urgent home or car repairs are just a few examples of situations that can arise without warning. Having a financial reserve allows you to handle these emergencies without resorting to loans or credit card debt, which often come with high interest rates.

2. **Stress Reduction:** Knowing you have a financial reserve can significantly reduce stress related to money matters. Financial uncertainty is one of the main causes of anxiety and stress. Having an emergency fund provides peace of mind, allowing you to focus on other important aspects of your life, such as health, family, and career.

3. **Investment Opportunities:** Having saved money also opens doors to investment opportunities. When you have a financial reserve, you can take advantage of investment opportunities that arise, such as buying stocks at low prices during a market downturn or purchasing a property at a discount. These opportunities can significantly increase your wealth over time.

4. **Future Planning:** Regular saving allows you to plan for the future with more confidence. Whether it's buying a home, funding your children's education, or planning for retirement, having a financial reserve helps ensure you can

achieve your long-term goals. Effective financial planning is essential for building a stable and prosperous life.

Examples of How Savings Can Help in Financial Emergencies

1. **Medical Expenses:** Imagine you or a family member needs emergency surgery. Without a financial reserve, you might be forced to take out a loan or use a credit card to cover the medical costs, resulting in significant debt. With savings, you can pay these expenses without compromising your financial stability.

2. **Job Loss:** Losing a job is one of the most stressful situations a person can face. Without a financial reserve, you might find yourself in a desperate situation, struggling to pay bills and maintain your standard of living. Having an emergency fund allows you to cover your basic expenses while you look for a new job, giving you time to find a position that truly aligns with your skills and interests.

3. **Urgent Repairs:** Unexpected home or car repairs can be extremely expensive. Without a financial reserve, you might be forced to delay these repairs, leading to even bigger and more costly problems in the future. With savings, you can handle these repairs immediately, avoiding additional complications.

4. **Business Opportunities:** Sometimes, business opportunities arise that require an initial investment. Without a financial reserve, you might miss out on these opportunities. Having savings allows you to take advantage of these opportunities, potentially increasing your income and wealth in the long term.

Building an Emergency Fund

Building an emergency fund is one of the most important steps to ensure your financial security. An emergency fund is a reserve of money set aside to cover unexpected expenses and financial emergencies. Having a well-structured emergency fund can make the difference between facing a financial crisis with confidence or falling into a cycle of debt.

How Much to Save

The amount of money you should save in your emergency fund can vary depending on your financial and personal situation. However, a general rule of thumb is to have the equivalent of three to six months of basic expenses saved. This includes costs such as rent or mortgage, utility bills, food, transportation, and other essential expenses.

1. **Three Months of Expenses:** If you have a stable income and a secure job, an emergency fund of three months of basic expenses may be sufficient. This will give you a safety net to handle short-term emergencies, such as car repairs or unexpected medical expenses.

2. **Six Months of Expenses:** If you have a variable income, such as freelancers or self-employed workers, or if your job is less secure, it is advisable to have an emergency fund of six months of basic expenses. This will give you more time to find a new source of income in case of job loss or other financial emergencies.

3. **More than Six Months of Expenses:** In some situations, it may be prudent to have an even larger emergency fund. For example, if you have dependents, such as children or elderly parents, or if you have recurring medical expenses, you may need a larger financial reserve to ensure you can cover all your needs in case of an emergency.

Where to Keep the Money

Accessibility and security are the two main factors to consider when deciding where to keep your emergency fund. You want the money to be easily accessible in case of an emergency, but you also want to ensure it is safe and protected from loss.

1. **Savings Account:** A savings account is one of the most common options for keeping an emergency fund. Savings accounts are secure and offer easy access to your money. Additionally, most savings accounts offer a small interest yield, which can help grow your emergency fund over time.

2. **Checking Account:** While checking accounts generally do not offer interest, they are extremely accessible. If you need to access your emergency fund quickly, a checking account can be a good option. However, it is important to ensure you do not spend this money on non-emergency expenses.

3. **Certificates of Deposit (CDs):** Certificates of deposit (CDs) are a safe option for keeping your emergency fund, especially if you do not need to access the money immediately. CDs generally offer higher interest rates than savings accounts but require you to keep the money invested for a fixed period. If you choose a CD, it is advisable to select one with a short term so you can access the money in case of an emergency.

4. **Money Market Funds:** Money market funds are a low-risk investment option that can offer a slightly higher yield than savings accounts. These funds invest in short-term securities and are generally considered safe. However, it is

important to check the fees and minimum balance requirements before investing.

Tips for Building an Emergency Fund

1. **Start Small and Be Consistent:** Building an emergency fund can seem like a daunting task, especially if you are starting from scratch. However, it is important to remember that every small contribution counts. Start by saving a small amount and gradually increase it as your financial situation allows. Consistency is key to building a solid emergency fund.

2. **Automate Your Savings:** Automating your savings can make the process of building an emergency fund easier and more efficient. Set up automatic transfers from your checking account to your savings account or other chosen savings vehicle. This ensures you are saving regularly without having to think about it.

3. **Reduce Unnecessary Expenses:** An effective way to increase your savings is to reduce unnecessary expenses. Review your budget and identify areas where you can cut costs. This may

include reducing dining out, canceling unused subscriptions, or finding ways to save on utility bills.

4. **Utilize Extra Income:** If you receive extra income, such as bonuses, tax refunds, or cash gifts, consider directing a portion or all of that money to your emergency fund. This can help quickly boost your savings.

5. **Review and Adjust Regularly:** Your financial situation may change over time, so it is important to review and adjust your emergency fund regularly. Ensure the amount you are saving is still adequate for your needs and make adjustments as necessary.

Conclusion

Saving and building an emergency fund are essential components of a healthy financial life. Having a financial reserve provides security in times of uncertainty, reduces stress, opens doors to investment opportunities, and allows for more effective future planning. By determining how much to save and where to keep your money, you can ensure you are prepared to face any financial emergency that may arise. With consistency and discipline, you can build a solid emergency fund that will give you the peace of mind and security needed to live a stable and prosperous financial life.

Chapter 5: Introduction to Investments

Investing is one of the most effective ways to build wealth over time. However, the world of investments can be complex and intimidating for beginners. This chapter aims to provide a comprehensive introduction to different types of investments and explain how to evaluate the risk and return of each. Understanding these concepts is fundamental to making informed decisions and building a diversified portfolio that meets your financial goals.

Types of Investments

There are several types of investments available, each with its own characteristics, advantages, and disadvantages. Let's explore some of the most common investments: stocks, bonds, real estate investment trusts (REITs), and cryptocurrencies.

Stocks

Definition and Characteristics: Stocks represent ownership in a company. When you buy a stock, you become a shareholder and, therefore, a partial owner of the company. Stocks are traded on stock exchanges, such as the New York Stock Exchange (NYSE) or NASDAQ.

Advantages:

- **Growth Potential:** Stocks have the potential to offer significant returns over time, especially if the company grows and becomes more profitable.

- **Dividends:** Some companies pay dividends, which are distributions of profits to shareholders. This can provide an additional source of income.

- **Liquidity:** Stocks are generally easy to buy and sell, meaning you can quickly convert your investment into cash if needed.

Disadvantages:

- **Volatility:** Stock prices can be highly volatile, rising and falling quickly based on factors such as company performance, economic conditions, and global events.

- **Risk of Loss:** There is a risk of losing part or all of your investment if the company performs poorly or goes bankrupt.

Investment Strategies:

- **Value Investing:** Focus on stocks that are undervalued by the market but have growth potential.

- **Growth Investing:** Focus on stocks of companies that are growing rapidly and have the potential to continue growing.

- **Dividend Investing:** Focus on stocks of companies that pay regular and consistent dividends.

Bonds

Definition and Characteristics: Bonds are debt instruments issued by governments, companies, or other entities to finance projects and operations. When you buy a bond, you are lending money to the issuer in exchange for regular interest payments and the repayment of the principal at maturity.

Advantages:

- **Fixed Income:** Bonds offer regular interest payments, which can provide a stable source of income.

- **Lower Risk:** Bonds are generally considered less risky than stocks, especially government bonds.

- **Diversification:** Including bonds in your portfolio can help diversify your investments and reduce overall risk.

Disadvantages:

- **Limited Return:** Bonds generally offer lower returns than stocks, especially during periods of low inflation.

- **Credit Risk:** There is a risk that the bond issuer may not be able to make interest payments or repay the principal at maturity.

Types of Bonds:

- **Government Bonds:** Issued by national governments and generally considered the safest investments.

- **Municipal Bonds:** Issued by local governments to finance public projects.

- **Corporate Bonds:** Issued by companies to finance operations and expansion projects.

Real Estate Investment Trusts (REITs)

Definition and Characteristics: REITs are investment vehicles that allow investors to buy shares in commercial real estate properties, such as shopping centers, office buildings, and warehouses. REITs are traded on stock exchanges, similar to stocks.

Advantages:

- **Diversification:** REITs allow investors to diversify their investments in real estate without the need to buy and manage properties directly.

- **Passive Income:** REITs typically distribute most of their rental income to investors in the form of dividends.

- **Accessibility:** Investing in REITs requires less initial capital than buying properties directly.

Disadvantages:

- **Market Risk:** The value of REITs can be affected by economic conditions and the real estate market.

- **Liquidity:** Although REITs are traded on stock exchanges, they can be less liquid than stocks, especially in smaller markets.

Types of REITs:

- **Income REITs:** Focused on generating stable and consistent rental income.

- **Development REITs:** Focused on developing new properties and selling or leasing them for profit.

- **Hybrid REITs:** Combine income and development strategies.

Cryptocurrencies

Definition and Characteristics: Cryptocurrencies are digital currencies that use cryptography to secure transactions and control the creation of new units. The most well-known cryptocurrencies include Bitcoin, Ethereum, and Ripple.

Advantages:

- **High Return Potential:** Cryptocurrencies have the potential to offer significant returns, especially during periods of high volatility.

- **Decentralization:** Cryptocurrencies are not controlled by governments or financial institutions, which can offer greater freedom and privacy.

- **Technological Innovation:** Investing in cryptocurrencies can provide exposure to emerging technologies, such as blockchain.

Disadvantages:

- **High Volatility:** Cryptocurrency prices can be extremely volatile, rising and falling quickly based on factors such as news, regulations, and market sentiment.

- **Security Risk:** Cryptocurrencies are vulnerable to hacks and fraud, and losing private keys can result in the permanent loss of funds.

- **Regulatory Uncertainty:** Cryptocurrency regulation is constantly evolving, which can create uncertainties and additional risks.

Investment Strategies:

- **Buy and Hold (HODL):** Buy cryptocurrencies and hold them long-term, regardless of price fluctuations.

- **Short-Term Trading:** Buy and sell cryptocurrencies based on short-term price movements.

- **Staking and Yield Farming:** Participate in cryptocurrency networks to earn additional rewards.

Risk and Return

Evaluating the risk and potential return of different investments is fundamental to building a balanced portfolio aligned with your financial goals. The relationship between risk and return is one of the most important concepts in finance, and understanding how to balance these factors can help you make more informed investment decisions.

Evaluating Risk

Risk is the possibility that the actual return on an investment will differ from the expected return. There are several types of risk that investors should consider:

1. **Market Risk:** Market risk is the possibility that the value of an investment will fall due to changes in market conditions. This can include fluctuations in stock prices, changes in interest rates, and variations in exchange rates.

2. **Credit Risk:** Credit risk is the possibility that the issuer of a bond will be unable to make interest payments or repay the principal at maturity. This is particularly relevant for corporate and municipal bonds.

3. **Liquidity Risk:** Liquidity risk is the possibility that you will be unable to sell an investment quickly without incurring a significant loss. This

can be a problem for less liquid investments, such as real estate and certain types of bonds.

4. **Operational Risk:** Operational risk is the possibility that internal problems within a company or organization, such as fraud or management failures, will affect the value of an investment.

5. **Regulatory Risk:** Regulatory risk is the possibility that changes in laws and regulations will affect the value of an investment. This is particularly relevant for highly regulated sectors, such as healthcare and energy.

Evaluating Return

Return is the reward you receive for taking on the risk of an investment. There are several ways to measure the return on an investment:

1. **Absolute Return:** Absolute return is the total gain or loss on an investment over a specific period. This can be measured in terms of monetary value or percentage.

2. **Relative Return:** Relative return is the performance of an investment compared to a benchmark index. This can help evaluate whether an investment is outperforming or underperforming the market.

3. **Risk-Adjusted Return:** Risk-adjusted return is a measure that takes into account the risk taken to achieve a certain return. This can include metrics such as the Sharpe Ratio, which compares the return of an investment to its volatility.

Relationship Between Risk and Return

The relationship between risk and return is a fundamental principle in finance. In general, investments with higher potential returns also come with higher risk. Conversely, safer investments tend to offer lower returns. The key to building a successful portfolio is finding a balance between risk and return that aligns with your financial goals and risk tolerance.

Practical Example: Consider two hypothetical investments: Stock X and Bond Y. Stock X has a potential annual return of 15% but also has high volatility, with its price fluctuating significantly over time. Bond Y, on the other hand, offers an annual return of 5% but is much more stable and predictable.

If you have a high risk tolerance and are looking to maximize your long-term returns, Stock X may be a suitable choice. However, if you prefer stability and are more concerned with protecting your capital, Bond Y may be a better option.

Risk and Return Chart

To illustrate the relationship between risk and return, consider the following table:

INVESTMENT TYPE	RISK (VOLATILITY)	EXPECTED RETURN
Stocks	High	High
Corporate Bonds	Medium	Medium
Government Bonds	Low	Low
Real Estate Investment Trusts (REITs)	Medium	Medium

INVESTMENT TYPE	RISK (VOLATILITY)	EXPECTED RETURN
Cryptocurrencies	Very High	Very High

In this chart, we can observe that:

- **Stocks:** Present high risk due to their volatility but also offer high expected returns.

- **Corporate Bonds:** Have medium risk and medium expected returns, serving as an intermediate option between stocks and government bonds.

- **Government Bonds:** Are considered low-risk investments with low expected returns but offer greater security.

- **REITs:** Offer medium risk and returns, providing diversification and passive income.

- **Cryptocurrencies:** Present the highest risk due to their high volatility but also have the potential to offer very high returns.

Balancing Risk and Return

To balance risk and return when building a portfolio, investors can use several strategies:

1. **Diversification:** Diversifying your investments is one of the most effective ways to reduce risk without sacrificing return. By spreading your investments across different asset classes, sectors, and geographies, you can reduce exposure to any specific risk.

2. **Asset Allocation:** Asset allocation involves dividing your portfolio among different types of investments, such as stocks, bonds, and real estate, based on your risk tolerance and financial goals. A well-planned asset allocation can help balance risk and return.

3. **Regular Rebalancing:** Regular rebalancing involves adjusting the composition of your portfolio to maintain your desired asset allocation. This may involve selling investments that have performed well and buying those that have underperformed to maintain balance.

4. **Fundamental and Technical Analysis:** Using fundamental and technical analysis can help

identify investments that offer a good balance between risk and return. Fundamental analysis involves evaluating a company's financial fundamentals, while technical analysis involves studying price and volume patterns.

5. **Investing in Funds:** Investing in mutual funds or ETFs (exchange-traded funds) can offer instant diversification and professional management, helping to balance risk and return. These funds typically invest in a wide range of assets, which can reduce overall portfolio risk.

Conclusion

Investing is a powerful tool for building wealth and achieving your financial goals. Understanding the different types of investments and how to evaluate the risk and return of each is fundamental to making informed decisions. By balancing risk and return and using strategies such as diversification and asset allocation, you can build a portfolio that meets your needs and financial objectives. Remember that investing is a long-term journey, and patience and discipline are essential for achieving

Chapter 6: Portfolio Diversification

Diversification is one of the most fundamental and effective strategies for risk management in investments. By spreading your investments across different assets, sectors, and geographies, you can reduce exposure to any specific risk and increase the likelihood of achieving more stable and consistent returns. This chapter explores the importance of diversification, the theory behind it, and practical strategies for implementing diversification in your portfolio.

Importance of Diversification

Risk Reduction

Diversification is essential because it helps reduce unsystematic risk, also known as specific or idiosyncratic risk. This type of risk is associated with a particular asset or company and can be mitigated by including a variety of assets in your portfolio. By diversifying, you avoid putting "all your eggs in one basket," meaning the negative performance of one investment can be offset by the positive performance of another.

Theory Behind Diversification: Modern portfolio theory, developed by Harry Markowitz in the 1950s, is the foundation of diversification. Markowitz demonstrated that a diversified portfolio could offer a higher expected return for a given level of risk or a lower risk for a given level of expected return. This is possible because the assets in a diversified portfolio are not perfectly correlated; that is, they do not move in the same direction at the same time.

Historical Example: During the 2008 financial crisis, many investors with portfolios concentrated in bank and financial institution stocks suffered significant losses. However, those with diversified portfolios, including government bonds, commodities, and stocks from less affected sectors like healthcare and consumer staples, managed to mitigate some of the losses. This illustrates how diversification can protect investments against market volatility.

Protection Against Market Volatility

Market volatility is an inevitable reality for all investors. However, diversification can help smooth out the market's ups and downs, providing more stable returns over time. When one asset or sector is down, another may be up, balancing the overall performance of the portfolio.

Historical Example: Consider the period from 2000 to 2002 when the dot-com bubble burst, leading to a significant decline in tech stock prices. Investors with portfolios concentrated in tech stocks suffered substantial losses. However, those with diversified portfolios, including bonds, real estate, and stocks from less affected sectors like energy and healthcare, managed to protect their investments against extreme market volatility.

Diversification Strategies

There are several approaches to diversifying an investment portfolio. Below, we discuss some of the most common and effective strategies.

Sector Diversification

Definition and Importance: Diversifying by sector involves investing in different sectors of the economy, such as technology, healthcare, finance, energy, consumer staples, and others. Each sector has its own characteristics and responds differently to economic, political, and technological changes.

Practical Example: An investor might allocate 20% of their portfolio to tech stocks, 20% to healthcare stocks, 20% to consumer staples stocks, 20% to energy stocks, and 20% to financial stocks. This way, if the tech sector faces difficulties, the negative impact on the portfolio can be offset by the positive performance of other sectors.

Case Study: During the COVID-19 pandemic in 2020, the technology and healthcare sectors performed exceptionally well, while sectors like energy and tourism suffered significant losses. Investors with sector-diversified portfolios managed to mitigate losses in negatively affected sectors by benefiting from the positive performance of the technology and healthcare sectors.

Geographic Diversification

Definition and Importance: Geographic diversification involves investing in different regions and countries. This can help reduce the risk associated with economic, political, or natural events affecting a specific region.

Practical Example: An investor might allocate 40% of their portfolio to U.S. stocks, 30% to European stocks, 20% to Asian stocks, and 10% to emerging market stocks. This way, if one region faces economic or political difficulties, the negative impact on the portfolio can be offset by the positive performance of other regions.

Case Study: During the European sovereign debt crisis from 2010 to 2012, many investors with portfolios concentrated in European stocks suffered significant losses. However, those with geographically diversified portfolios, including U.S., Asian, and emerging market stocks, managed to mitigate some of the losses.

Asset Class Diversification

Definition and Importance: Diversifying by asset class involves investing in different types of assets, such as stocks, bonds, real estate, commodities, and cryptocurrencies. Each asset class has its own risk and return characteristics and responds differently to economic and market changes.

Practical Example: An investor might allocate 40% of their portfolio to stocks, 30% to bonds, 20% to real estate, and 10% to commodities. This way, if the stock market faces difficulties, the negative impact on the portfolio can be offset by the positive performance of bonds, real estate, and commodities.

Case Study: During the 2008 financial crisis, many investors with portfolios concentrated in stocks suffered significant losses. However, those with portfolios diversified by asset class, including government bonds, real estate, and commodities like gold, managed to mitigate some of the losses.

Investment Style Diversification

Definition and Importance: Diversifying by investment style involves investing in different investment styles, such as growth, value, dividends, and small caps. Each investment style has its own characteristics and responds differently to economic and market changes.

Practical Example: An investor might allocate 25% of their portfolio to growth stocks, 25% to value stocks, 25% to dividend stocks, and 25% to small-cap stocks. This way, if one investment style faces difficulties, the negative impact on the portfolio can be offset by the positive performance of other styles.

Case Study: During the post-2008 financial crisis economic recovery, growth stocks, especially in the technology sector, performed exceptionally well. Investors with portfolios diversified by investment style managed to benefit from the positive performance of growth stocks while mitigating the risk associated with other investment styles.

Time Horizon Diversification

Definition and Importance: Diversifying by time horizon involves investing in assets with different time horizons, such as short, medium, and long-term. This can help balance risk and return over time and meet different financial goals.

Practical Example: An investor might allocate 30% of their portfolio to short-term investments, such as short-term bonds and savings accounts, 40% to medium-term investments, such as medium-term bonds and mutual funds, and 30% to long-term investments, such as stocks and real estate. This way, the investor can meet different financial goals and balance risk and return over time.

Case Study: During the 2008 financial crisis, many investors with portfolios concentrated in long-term investments, such as stocks, suffered significant losses. However, those with portfolios diversified by time horizon, including short and medium-term investments, managed to mitigate some of the losses and meet different financial goals.

Implementing Diversification

Implementing diversification in your portfolio involves several steps, including defining financial goals, assessing your risk tolerance, and selecting diversified assets. Below, we discuss some of the most important steps for implementing diversification in your portfolio.

Defining Financial Goals

Before diversifying your portfolio, it is important to define your financial goals. This can include short-term goals, such as saving for a trip or buying a car, medium-term goals, such as saving for children's education, and long-term goals, such as saving for retirement.

Practical Example: An investor might define the following financial goals:

- **Short-Term:** Save $10,000 for a trip in two years.
- **Medium-Term:** Save $50,000 for children's education in ten years.
- **Long-Term:** Save $500,000 for retirement in thirty years.

Assessing Risk Tolerance

Risk tolerance is an investor's ability and willingness to take on risks. This can vary based on factors such as age, financial situation, time horizon, and financial goals. Assessing your risk tolerance is fundamental to selecting assets that align with your risk profile.

Practical Example: A young investor with a long time horizon and high risk tolerance might opt for a more aggressive portfolio with a higher allocation to stocks and cryptocurrencies. On the other hand, an older investor nearing retirement with a low risk tolerance might opt for a more conservative portfolio with a higher allocation to bonds and real estate.

Selecting Diversified Assets

Selecting diversified assets involves choosing a variety of assets that align with your financial goals and risk tolerance. This can include stocks, bonds, real estate, commodities, and cryptocurrencies, among others.

Practical Example: An investor might select the following assets to diversify their portfolio:

- **Stocks:** 40% of the portfolio, including stocks from different sectors and regions.

- **Bonds:** 30% of the portfolio, including government and corporate bonds.

- **Real Estate:** 20% of the portfolio, including REITs and direct properties.

- **Commodities:** 5% of the portfolio, including gold and oil.

- **Cryptocurrencies:** 5% of the portfolio, including Bitcoin and Ethereum.

Monitoring and Rebalancing

Regularly monitoring and rebalancing your portfolio is fundamental to maintaining diversification and ensuring your portfolio aligns with your financial goals and risk tolerance. Rebalancing involves adjusting the composition of your portfolio to maintain your desired asset allocation.

Practical Example: An investor might monitor their portfolio quarterly and rebalance annually. If the performance of a specific asset, such as stocks, is exceptional, the allocation to stocks might increase beyond the desired allocation. In this case, the investor might sell some stocks and buy other assets, such as bonds and real estate, to maintain diversification.

Conclusion

Diversification is a fundamental strategy for risk management in investments. By spreading your investments across different assets, sectors, geographies, investment styles, and time horizons, you can reduce exposure to any specific risk and increase the likelihood of achieving more stable and consistent returns. Implementing diversification in your portfolio involves defining financial goals, assessing your risk tolerance, selecting diversified assets, and regularly monitoring and rebalancing your portfolio. With a diversified approach, you can protect your investments against market volatility and achieve your long-term financial goals.

Chapter 7: Investments for Beginners

Investing can seem like a daunting task, especially for those starting with little money. However, with the right strategies and a bit of knowledge, anyone can begin investing and build a solid portfolio over time. This chapter will provide detailed guidance on how to start investing with little money, identify accessible investment opportunities, and avoid common beginner mistakes. Additionally, we will discuss the best platforms and apps that make investing easier for beginners.

Getting Started

How to Start Investing with Little Money

Many people believe that a large sum of money is necessary to start investing, but this is not true. With the advent of financial technologies and accessible investment platforms, it is possible to start investing with very small amounts. Here are some steps to begin investing with little money:

1. **Define Your Financial Goals:** Before you start investing, it is important to define your financial goals. Ask yourself what you hope to achieve with your investments. Your goals might include saving for retirement, buying a home, paying for your children's education, or simply increasing your wealth over time. Defining clear goals will help guide your investment decisions.

2. **Create an Emergency Fund:** Before investing, it is essential to have an emergency fund. An emergency fund is a reserve of money that can cover unexpected expenses, such as car repairs, medical bills, or job loss. It is recommended to have at least three to six months of living expenses in an emergency fund. This ensures that you do not need to sell your investments at inopportune times to cover unexpected expenses.

3. **Start with Low-Cost Investments:** There are several low-cost investment options that are ideal for beginners. Some of these options include:

- **Index Funds:** Index funds are mutual funds or ETFs (exchange-traded funds) that track a specific index, such as the S&P 500. They offer instant diversification and generally have lower fees than actively managed funds.

- **Fractional Shares:** Some brokers allow you to buy fractional shares, meaning you can purchase a fraction of a share instead of a whole share. This allows you to invest in high-value companies like Amazon or Google with smaller amounts of money.

- **Real Estate Investment Trusts (REITs):** REITs are companies that own and operate income-generating real estate. They allow you to invest in real estate without having to buy physical properties. REITs typically pay regular dividends, which can be a source of passive income.

4. **Automate Your Investments:** Automating your investments is an effective way to ensure

that you continue investing regularly, regardless of market fluctuations. Many brokers and investment apps allow you to set up automatic transfers from your bank account to your investment account. This helps maintain discipline and build your portfolio over time.

5. **Continuously Educate Yourself:** The world of investing is constantly evolving, and it is important to keep learning. There are many resources available, such as books, blogs, podcasts, and online courses, that can help you expand your knowledge about investing. The more you know, the more confident you will feel in making investment decisions.

Identifying Accessible Investment Opportunities

Identifying accessible investment opportunities is crucial for beginners starting with little money. Here are some tips to help you find these opportunities:

1. **Research and Compare Brokers:** Not all brokers are the same, and some are more

suitable for beginners than others. Look for brokers that offer accounts with no minimum opening balance, low or zero commissions, and access to a wide range of investment products. Some popular brokers for beginners include Robinhood, E*TRADE, Charles Schwab, and Fidelity.

2. **Utilize Micro-Investing Apps:** Micro-investing apps, such as Acorns, Stash, and Betterment, allow you to invest small amounts of money regularly. These apps typically round up your daily purchases to the nearest dollar and invest the difference in a diversified portfolio. This makes it easy to start investing, even with very small amounts.

3. **Invest in Index Funds and ETFs:** As mentioned earlier, index funds and ETFs are low-cost investment options that offer instant diversification. They are ideal for beginners because they do not require you to pick individual stocks, which can be risky and time-consuming. Instead, you can invest in a fund that

tracks a broad index, such as the S&P 500, and gain exposure to hundreds of companies with a single purchase.

4. **Consider Automated Investments:** Automated investment platforms, also known as robo-advisors, are an excellent option for beginners. These platforms, such as Betterment, Wealthfront, and Ellevest, use algorithms to create and manage a diversified portfolio based on your financial goals and risk tolerance. They typically charge lower fees than traditional financial advisors and offer a convenient way to start investing.

5. **Participate in Employer-Sponsored Retirement Plans:** If your employer offers a retirement plan, such as a 401(k) in the United States, take advantage of this opportunity. Many employers offer matching contributions, which is essentially free money. Contributing to an employer-sponsored retirement plan is an effective way to start investing and take advantage of tax benefits.

Avoiding Common Beginner Mistakes

Investing can be intimidating, and it is easy to make mistakes, especially when you are just starting out. Here are some common mistakes that beginners should avoid:

1. **Not Diversifying:** One of the most common mistakes beginners make is not diversifying their investments. Putting all your money into a single stock or sector can be risky. Diversifying your portfolio helps spread risk and increases the likelihood of stable returns.

2. **Trying to Time the Market:** Trying to predict the highs and lows of the market is a risky and often ineffective strategy. Instead, focus on investing regularly and maintaining a long-term perspective. Systematic investing, such as dollar-cost averaging, can help mitigate the impact of market volatility.

3. **Ignoring Fees and Costs:** Investment fees and costs can erode your returns over time. Make sure you understand all the fees associated with your investments, including brokerage

commissions, fund management fees, and advisory fees. Choose low-cost investments whenever possible.

4. **Making Emotional Decisions:** The stock market can be volatile, and it is easy to let emotions influence your investment decisions. Avoid making impulsive decisions based on fear or greed. Stick to your investment plan and remember that investing is a marathon, not a sprint.

5. **Not Reassessing and Rebalancing the Portfolio:** As the market fluctuates, the composition of your portfolio can change. It is important to reassess and rebalance your portfolio regularly to ensure it remains aligned with your financial goals and risk tolerance. This may involve selling assets that have appreciated and buying assets that have depreciated to maintain your desired asset allocation.

Investment Platforms

There are many platforms and apps that make investing easier for beginners. Below, we discuss some of the best options, their features and benefits, as well as reviews and comparisons to help you choose the best platform for your needs.

Online Brokers

1. **Robinhood:**

    - **Features:** Robinhood is an online broker that offers commission-free trading of stocks, ETFs, options, and cryptocurrencies. The platform is known for its user-friendly interface, making it ideal for beginners.

    - **Benefits:** No trading commissions, access to a wide range of investment products, intuitive interface.

    - **Review:** Robinhood is an excellent option for beginners who want to start investing with little money and without paying commissions. However, the platform has been criticized for its lack of educational resources and limited customer support.

2. **E*TRADE:**

    - **Features:** E*TRADE offers a wide range of investment products, including stocks, ETFs, options, bonds, and mutual funds. The platform also provides research tools and educational resources to help investors make informed decisions.

    - **Benefits:** Access to a wide range of investment products, robust research tools, comprehensive educational resources.

    - **Review:** E*TRADE is an excellent option for beginners who want access to a wide range of investment products and research tools. The platform may be a bit more complex than other options, but it offers many useful features.

3. **Charles Schwab:**

    - **Features:** Charles Schwab offers a wide range of investment products, including stocks, ETFs, options, bonds, and mutual funds. The platform also provides educational resources, research tools, and high-quality customer support.

- **Benefits:** Access to a wide range of investment products, comprehensive educational resources, high-quality customer support.

- **Review:** Charles Schwab is an excellent option for beginners who want access to a wide range of investment products and high-quality customer support. The platform is known for its reliability and comprehensive educational resources.

4. **Fidelity:**

    - **Features:** Fidelity offers a wide range of investment products, including stocks, ETFs, options, bonds, and mutual funds. The platform also provides educational resources, research tools, and high-quality customer support.

- **Benefits:** Access to a wide range of investment products, comprehensive educational resources, high-quality customer support.

- **Review:** Fidelity is an excellent option for beginners who want access to a wide range of investment products and high-quality customer support. The platform is known for its reliability and comprehensive educational resources.

Micro-Investing Apps

1. **Acorns:**

    - **Features:** Acorns is a micro-investing app that rounds up your daily purchases to the nearest dollar and invests the difference in a diversified portfolio of ETFs. The app also offers retirement accounts and investment accounts for kids.

- **Benefits:** Automated investing, diversified portfolio, retirement accounts, and investment accounts for kids.

- **Review:** Acorns is an excellent option for beginners who want to start investing with small amounts of money. The app makes automated investing easy and provides a convenient way to build a diversified portfolio.

2. **Stash:**

    - **Features:** Stash is a micro-investing app that allows you to invest in fractional shares and ETFs with small amounts of money. The app also provides educational resources and financial planning tools.

    - **Benefits:** Investment in fractional shares, educational resources, financial planning tools.

    - **Review:** Stash is an excellent option for beginners who want to invest in fractional shares and ETFs with small amounts of money. The app offers useful educational resources and financial planning tools to help investors make informed decisions.

3. **Betterment:**

    - **Features:** Betterment is an automated investment platform (robo-advisor) that creates and manages a diversified portfolio based on your financial goals and risk tolerance. The platform also offers retirement accounts and investment accounts for kids.

    - **Benefits:** Automated investing, diversified portfolio, retirement accounts, and investment accounts for kids.

    - **Review:** Betterment is an excellent option for beginners who want an automated approach to investing. The platform makes it easy to create and manage a diversified portfolio and provides a convenient way to achieve your financial goals.

Comparison of Investment Platforms

Below is a comparison of the top investment platforms for beginners, based on their features, benefits, and reviews:

PLATFORM	FEATURES	BENEFITS	REVIEW
Robinhood	Commission-free trading, user-friendly interface	No trading commissions, intuitive interface	Excellent for beginners, but lacks educational resources and limited customer support
E*TRADE	Wide range of products, research tools	Access to many products, educational resources	Excellent for beginners who want robust research tools

PLATFORM	FEATURES	BENEFITS	REVIEW
Charles Schwab	Wide range of products, high-quality support	Comprehensive educational resources, high-quality support	Excellent for beginners who want high-quality customer support
Fidelity	Wide range of products, high-quality support	Comprehensive educational resources, high-quality support	Excellent for beginners who want high-quality customer support
Acorns	Automated investing, diversified portfolio	Automated investing, retirement accounts	Excellent for beginners who want to start investing with small amounts

PLATFORM	FEATURES	BENEFITS	REVIEW
Stash	Fractional shares, educational resources	Fractional shares, financial planning tools	Excellent for beginners who want to invest in fractional shares and ETFs
Betterment	Automated investing, diversified portfolio	Automated investing, retirement accounts	Excellent for beginners who want an automated approach to investing

Conclusion

Investing can seem intimidating for beginners, especially when starting with little money. However, with the right strategies and the use of accessible investment platforms, anyone can begin investing and build a solid portfolio over time. This chapter provided detailed guidance on how to start investing with little money, identify accessible investment opportunities, and avoid common beginner mistakes. Additionally, we discussed the best platforms and apps that make investing easier for beginners, helping you choose the best option for your needs. With a disciplined and educated approach, you can achieve your financial goals and build wealth over time.

Chapter 8: Advanced Investments

Investing at an advanced level requires a deeper understanding of analysis techniques and investment strategies. This chapter will cover two main methods of evaluating stocks and other assets: fundamental analysis and technical analysis. Additionally, we will discuss different investment strategies, such as value investing, growth investing, and dividend investing, explaining how each works and their respective advantages and disadvantages. We will use examples and charts to illustrate these methods and strategies, helping you make more informed investment decisions.

Introduction: The Crucial Difference Between Price and Value

To understand the crucial difference between price and value, something intrinsic for anyone looking to invest, it is necessary to address the different perspectives of investment schools. Confusing price with value can lead intelligent people to make poor financial decisions. Simply put, value is what an asset or service is truly worth, while price is what you pay for it. Warren Buffet, one of the world's greatest investors, defined price as what you pay and value as what you get.

Imagine a dire situation, such as a robbery, where you are left with only a watch that cost $1,000 at the time of purchase. Without a wallet, money, or phone, you decide to trade the watch for a $15 cab ride. At that moment, the watch is worth the $1,000 paid, but its real value is much lower due to the emergency situation. This example illustrates how the acquisition price of an asset can drastically differ from its value in specific situations.

Investor vs. Speculator

It is important to emphasize that investors and speculators are two distinct classes of people who participate in the financial market. Among investors, there are different schools of stock analysis, with the two main ones being Value Investing and Buy and Hold. Both have a long-term perspective and can be used complementarily, adapting their teachings to each type of investment and market moment.

Value Investing

Value Investing is an approach followed by great investors like Warren Buffet and his mentor, Benjamin Graham. This investment school is based on the idea that the market often confuses price with value, not pricing stocks correctly. Value investors try to find market asymmetries and buy good stocks at prices lower than their actual worth.

The main indicators used in Value Investing relate to the stock price, such as the P/B (Price to Book Value) and P/E (Price to Earnings) ratios. The P/B ratio involves dividing the stock price by its book value. Benjamin Graham said that a good investment would be one where the P/B ratio is less than 1 or just above it.

Warren Buffet used to say that the ideal was to buy bad companies at excellent prices. He used the term "cigar butts" to describe stocks that, even though they had been smoked, could still give one more puff. Currently, Buffet has changed his perspective and now looks for excellent companies at good prices, rather than bad companies at excellent prices. In the stock market, prices are formed based on supply and demand, allowing investors to find asymmetries and good companies at impressive prices.

Buy and Hold

The Buy and Hold investment school is based on the premise that the market has already priced all items efficiently. Investors using this method believe that with millions of investors analyzing numbers daily, it is unlikely to discover something new on their own. Some radicals of this theory are so convinced of the market's exact pricing that they do not admit that price asymmetries can occur even during crises.

The main philosophy of Buy and Hold is to buy a stock and hold it. A holder only sells their stocks if the company's fundamentals change. Otherwise, there are no exceptions. The profit comes only from dividends. One of the great icons of this philosophy is the billionaire Luiz Barsi Filho, the largest individual investor in Brazil.

For holders, only profitable companies are of interest. The older the company, the better the evaluation. They do not necessarily worry about the price paid for the stocks but rather the consistency of profits over time.

They do not usually work with opportunity reserves and do not stop contributions even during crises. In their view, waiting is almost always more advantageous than selling.

Comparison Between Value Investing and Buy and Hold

Both investment schools have excellent results. Luiz Barsi, for example, claims not to need an opportunity reserve because he receives millions just in dividends. However, most people do not have similar receipts, making the opportunity reserve absolutely important. It is sensible to try to condense the ideals of both schools, maintaining an opportunity reserve to take advantage of crises and buy stocks below their fair price.

Technology companies like Facebook, WhatsApp, and Uber are examples of companies that started with losses but eventually managed to grow or present growth projections. A classic Buy and Hold investor would never invest in these "potential" companies.

Fundamental Criteria for Choosing Companies

To invest successfully, it is crucial to choose companies based on fundamental criteria, such as:

- **Competitiveness:** Choose companies that are leaders in their sectors.

- **Profitability:** Invest in profitable companies.

- **Debt:** Invest in companies without debt or with controlled debt.

- **Fair Price:** Choose companies that are not being traded far above their fair value.

- **ROE (Return on Equity):** Check if the company's return on equity is good.

- **Net Margins:** Look for companies with consistent and positive net margins.

Investment Simulation

To illustrate the importance of detailed analysis and diversification, let's simulate an investment of $10,000 in 10 different companies. Imagine that company G went bankrupt, causing you to lose all your money. Company I lost half its value ($5,000), even with dividends during the period. However, we have company J that appreciated by 40%, H by 56%, company A by 113%, and B by 433%. C expanded by 2700%, and D by an incredible 3500%. E appreciated by 87%, and F by 200%. Overall, the total gain during the period was $777,600.

This simulation shows that even with companies that lost value or went bankrupt, the overall portfolio growth is undeniable. The simulation considered only single contributions, without additional investments over time, relying solely on the power of compound interest.

Fundamental and Technical Analysis

Fundamental Analysis

Fundamental analysis is a comprehensive and detailed approach that aims to assess the intrinsic value of an asset by considering a wide range of economic, financial, qualitative, and quantitative factors. The main goal is to determine whether an asset is undervalued or overvalued relative to its current market price, providing a solid foundation for informed investment decisions. Below, we explore the key components of fundamental analysis in greater depth.

1. Financial Statement Analysis

Financial statements are the foundation of fundamental analysis, providing a detailed view of a company's financial health and performance. The main financial statements include:

- **Balance Sheet:** The balance sheet provides an overview of a company's assets, liabilities, and equity at a specific point in time. It is divided into three main sections:

    - **Assets:** Include current assets (such as cash, accounts receivable, and inventory) and non-current assets (such as property, plant, and equipment).

    - **Liabilities:** Include current liabilities (such as accounts payable and short-term debt) and non-current liabilities (such as long-term debt).

    - **Equity:** Represents the difference between assets and liabilities, reflecting the residual value belonging to shareholders.

Example Analysis: By analyzing the balance sheet of a company like Coca-Cola, an investor can observe the ratio of current assets to current liabilities to assess the company's liquidity. Additionally, analyzing long-term debt relative to equity can provide insights into the company's financial leverage.

- **Income Statement:** The income statement, also known as the profit and loss statement, shows a company's revenues, expenses, and profits over a period. It is divided into several sections:

    - **Revenues:** Include sales of products and services.

    - **Cost of Goods Sold (COGS):** Include direct costs associated with producing the goods sold.

    - **Operating Expenses:** Include selling, general, and administrative expenses.

    - **Operating Income:** Calculated by subtracting operating expenses from revenues.

- **Net Income:** The final profit after deducting all expenses, including taxes and interest.

Example Analysis: By analyzing the income statement of a company like Apple, an investor can observe the operating profit margin to evaluate the company's efficiency in controlling costs. Analyzing revenue growth over time can also provide insights into the demand for the company's products and services.

- **Cash Flow Statement:** The cash flow statement shows a company's cash inflows and outflows, divided into three main categories:

    - **Operating Activities:** Include cash flows generated by the company's core operations.

    - **Investing Activities:** Include cash flows related to the purchase and sale of long-term assets.

    - **Financing Activities:** Include cash flows related to borrowing, issuing shares, and paying dividends.

Example Analysis: By analyzing the cash flow statement of a company like Amazon, an investor can observe the company's ability to generate cash from its core operations. Analyzing investing activities can provide insights into the company's expansion plans, while financing activities can reveal the company's capital strategy.

2. **Financial Ratios**

Financial ratios are essential metrics in fundamental analysis, providing a quantitative view of a company's performance and financial health. Some of the key ratios include:

- **P/E (Price/Earnings):** The P/E ratio is calculated by dividing the stock price by earnings per share (EPS). It helps evaluate whether a stock is expensive or cheap relative to its earnings.

Example Analysis: If the P/E ratio of Microsoft is significantly lower than the average P/E ratio of the technology sector, it may indicate that the stock is undervalued relative to its earnings.

- **P/B (Price/Book Value):** The P/B ratio is calculated by dividing the stock price by the book value per share (BVPS). It helps evaluate whether a stock is expensive or cheap relative to its book value.

Example Analysis: If the P/B ratio of JPMorgan Chase is less than 1, it may indicate that the stock is being traded below the company's book value, potentially representing a buying opportunity.

- **ROE (Return on Equity):** ROE is calculated by dividing net income by equity. It helps evaluate the company's efficiency in generating profits from shareholders' equity.

Example Analysis: A high ROE for a company like Johnson & Johnson may indicate efficient management and a good ability to generate returns for shareholders.

- **ROA (Return on Assets):** ROA is calculated by dividing net income by total assets. It helps evaluate the company's efficiency in generating profits from its assets.

Example Analysis: A high ROA for a company like Procter & Gamble may indicate efficient use of the company's assets to generate profits.

3. **Sector and Macroeconomic Analysis**

Sector and macroeconomic analysis provide a broader context for evaluating a company, considering external factors that may impact its performance.

- **Sector Analysis:** Sector analysis involves evaluating the performance and prospects of the sector in which the company operates. This includes analyzing competition, market demand, and sector trends.

Example Analysis: When analyzing the technology sector, an investor may observe the growth in demand for cloud services and artificial intelligence, identifying companies like Microsoft that are well-positioned to benefit from these trends.

- **Macroeconomic Analysis:** Macroeconomic analysis involves evaluating the impact of macroeconomic factors, such as interest rates, inflation, economic growth, and government policies, on the company's performance.

Example Analysis: In a declining interest rate environment, companies in the real estate sector, like Zillow, may benefit from lower financing costs and increased demand for properties.

4. **Valuation**

Valuation is the process of determining a company's intrinsic value using different valuation methods.

- **Discounted Cash Flow (DCF):** The DCF method estimates a company's intrinsic value based on projected future cash flows, discounted at an appropriate discount rate. It helps determine whether a stock is undervalued or overvalued.

Example Analysis: By performing a DCF analysis for a company like Tesla, an investor can project future cash flows based on historical revenue growth and profit margins, discounting these flows at a rate that reflects the investment's risk.

- **Market Multiples:** Comparing a company's market multiples (such as P/E, P/B, EV/EBITDA) with those of similar companies in the same sector helps evaluate whether the company is being traded at a fair price relative to its peers.

Example Analysis: Comparing the EV/EBITDA of a company like Walmart with other companies in the retail sector can provide insights into whether the stock is undervalued or overvalued relative to its competitors.

Technical Analysis

Technical analysis is an approach that evaluates the price behavior and trading volumes of an asset using charts and technical indicators. The goal is to identify patterns and trends that may predict future price movements. Here are the main components of technical analysis:

1. **Price Charts:**
    - **Line Chart:** Shows the closing price of an asset over time. It is useful for identifying general trends.

- **Bar Chart:** Shows the opening, closing, high, and low prices of an asset over a specific period. It is useful for analyzing volatility and the strength of price movements.

- **Candlestick Chart:** Similar to the bar chart but with a clearer visual representation of price variations. It is widely used to identify reversal and continuation patterns.

2. **Technical Indicators:**

    - **Moving Averages:** Moving averages smooth out price data to identify trends. Simple moving averages (SMA) and exponential moving averages (EMA) are the most common.

    - **Relative Strength Index (RSI):** The RSI measures the speed and change of price movements. An RSI above 70 indicates that an asset is overbought, while an RSI below 30 indicates that it is oversold.

- **MACD (Moving Average Convergence Divergence):** The MACD is a trend-following indicator that shows the relationship between two moving averages. It helps identify changes in the direction and strength of a trend.
- **Bollinger Bands:** Bollinger Bands consist of a moving average and two standard deviation lines above and below it. They help identify overbought and oversold levels.

3. **Chart Patterns:**

    - **Continuation Patterns:** Patterns like flags, pennants, and triangles indicate that the current trend is likely to continue.
    - **Reversal Patterns:** Patterns like head and shoulders, double top, and double bottom indicate that the current trend is likely to reverse.

4. **Trading Volume:**

- **Volume Analysis:** Trading volume is an important indicator of trend strength. An increase in volume confirms the trend's strength, while a decrease in volume may indicate an imminent reversal.

Examples and Charts

To illustrate fundamental and technical analysis methods, let's use practical examples and charts.

Example of Fundamental Analysis: Let's consider the fictional company "ABC Corp."

- **Balance Sheet:**
    - **Total Assets:** $1,000,000
    - **Total Liabilities:** $500,000
    - **Equity:** $500,000
- **Income Statement:**
    - **Net Revenue:** $800,000
    - **Cost of Goods Sold:** $400,000
    - **Gross Profit:** $400,000
    - **Operating Expenses:** $200,000

- **Operating Income:** $200,000
- **Net Income:** $150,000
- **Financial Ratios:**
  - **P/E:** 10 (Stock Price: $15.00, EPS: $1.50)
  - **P/B:** 1.5 (Stock Price: $15.00, BVPS: $10.00)
  - **ROE:** 30% (Net Income: $150,000, Equity: $500,000)
  - **ROA:** 15% (Net Income: $150,000, Total Assets: $1,000,000)

Example of Technical Analysis: Let's consider the price chart of the fictional company "XYZ Corp."

- **Candlestick Chart:**

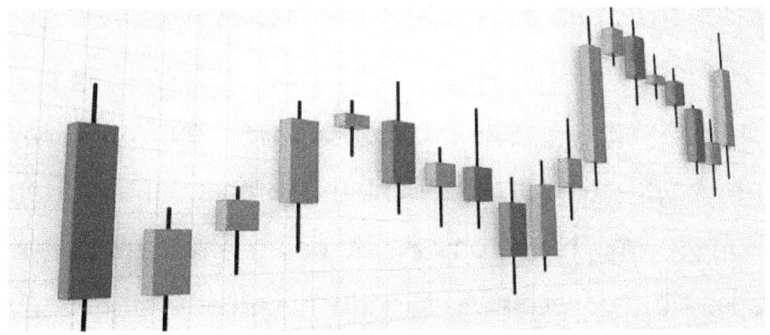

- **Technical Indicators:**

- **50-Day SMA:** $20.00
- **200-Day SMA:** $18.00
- **RSI:** 65
- **MACD:** MACD line (12,26,9) crossing above the signal line
- **Chart Patterns:**
  - **Ascending Triangle:** Indicates a possible continuation of the uptrend.

Investment Strategies

Value Investing

Value investing is a strategy that involves buying stocks that are undervalued relative to their intrinsic value. Value investors believe that the market will eventually recognize the true value of these stocks, resulting in a price increase. This approach was popularized by renowned investors like Benjamin Graham and Warren Buffett, who have consistently demonstrated that it is possible to achieve superior market returns by identifying and buying undervalued stocks. Below, we explore the key components of value investing in greater depth.

1. **Identifying Undervalued Stocks**

Identifying undervalued stocks is the first step in value investing. This involves a detailed analysis of the company's fundamentals to determine whether the current stock price is below its intrinsic value.

- **Valuation Indicators:** Valuation indicators are essential tools for identifying undervalued stocks. Some of the key indicators include:

    - **P/E (Price/Earnings):** Calculated by dividing the stock price by earnings per share (EPS). A low P/E may indicate that the stock is undervalued relative to its earnings.

    - **P/B (Price/Book Value):** Calculated by dividing the stock price by the book value per share (BVPS). A low P/B may indicate that the stock is being traded below its book value.

- **EV/EBITDA (Enterprise Value/EBITDA):** Calculated by dividing the enterprise value (market capitalization + net debt) by EBITDA (earnings before interest, taxes, depreciation, and amortization). A low EV/EBITDA may indicate that the company is undervalued relative to its operating cash flow.

- **Financial Statement Analysis:** Analyzing financial statements is crucial for assessing the company's financial health. This includes:

    - **Balance Sheet:** Evaluating the company's liquidity, leverage, and capital structure.

    - **Income Statement:** Analyzing profitability, profit margins, and operational efficiency.

    - **Cash Flow Statement:** Evaluating the company's ability to generate cash and finance its operations.

Example Analysis: By analyzing the fictional company "DEF Corp.," an investor may observe the following valuation indicators:

- P/E: 8 (Stock Price: $16.00, EPS: $2.00)
- P/B: 1.2 (Stock Price: $16.00, BVPS: $13.33)

Additionally, the analysis of financial statements reveals:

- **Net Revenue:** $1,000,000
- **Net Income:** $200,000
- **Equity:** $1,000,000

2. Margin of Safety

The margin of safety is a central concept in value investing, introduced by Benjamin Graham. It involves buying stocks at a significant discount to their intrinsic value to protect against valuation errors and market uncertainties.

Buying at a Discount

Purchasing at a discount provides a margin of safety that reduces the risk of permanent capital loss. This is especially important in a volatile market where stock prices can fluctuate significantly.

Example Analysis: For the company "DEF Corp.," the estimated intrinsic value is $25.00 per share. If the purchase price is $16.00, this represents a 36% discount, providing a substantial margin of safety.

3. Patience and Long-Term Perspective

Value investing requires patience and a long-term perspective. Value investors are willing to hold onto stocks for an extended period, allowing the market to recognize the company's intrinsic value.

Long-Term Investment

Holding stocks for a long period allows the investor to benefit from profit growth and the gradual recognition of intrinsic value by the market. This also reduces the impact of short-term price fluctuations.

Example Analysis: An investor who bought shares of "DEF Corp." at $16.00 may need to wait several years for the market to recognize the intrinsic value of $25.00.

During this period, the investor can benefit from dividends and profit growth of the company.

Advantages and Disadvantages of Value Investing

Advantages

- **Potential for High Returns:** When the market corrects the undervaluation, value investors can achieve significant returns.

- **Lower Risk of Permanent Capital Loss:** The margin of safety reduces the risk of permanent capital loss, providing protection against valuation errors and market uncertainties.

Disadvantages

- **Time for Recognition of Intrinsic Value:** It may take time for the market to recognize the intrinsic value, requiring patience from the investor.

- **Detailed Analysis and Understanding of Fundamentals:** It requires detailed analysis and a deep understanding of the company's fundamentals, which can be challenging for inexperienced investors.

Case Study: Fictional Company "DEF Corp."

Let's consider the fictional company "DEF Corp." to illustrate the application of value investing.

Valuation Indicators

- **P/E:** 8 (Stock Price: $16.00, EPS: $2.00)
- **P/B:** 1.2 (Stock Price: $16.00, BVPS: $13.33)

Financial Statement Analysis

- **Net Revenue:** $1,000,000
- **Net Income:** $200,000
- **Equity:** $1,000,000

Margin of Safety

- **Estimated Intrinsic Value:** $25.00
- **Purchase Price:** $16.00 (36% Discount)

Growth Investing

Growth investing is a strategy that involves buying stocks of companies that are growing rapidly and have the potential to continue growing at above-average market rates. Growth investors are willing to pay a premium for stocks of companies with strong growth potential, believing that future profit increases will justify the higher price paid today. This approach can be highly lucrative but also involves significant risks. Below, we explore the key components of growth investing in greater depth.

1. Identifying Growth Companies

Identifying growth companies is the first crucial step in this strategy. This involves analyzing various factors that indicate a company's future growth potential.

Growth Rates

Growth companies typically exhibit high growth rates in revenue, profit, and cash flow. These indicators signal that the company is expanding its operations and gaining market share.

- **Revenue Growth:** Indicates the company's ability to increase its sales over time. Revenue growth rates above the industry average are a good sign of a growth company.

- **Profit Growth:** Reflects the company's ability to increase its net profits. Growth companies typically reinvest a significant portion of their profits to finance future expansion.

- **Cash Flow Growth:** Increasing operating cash flow is an indicator that the company is generating enough cash to sustain its operations and finance new projects.

Innovation and Competitive Advantage

Growth companies often stand out for their ability to innovate and maintain a sustainable competitive advantage. This can include:

- **Innovative Product:** Companies that develop innovative products or services that meet unmet market needs have greater growth potential.

- **Competitive Advantage:** Companies with competitive advantages, such as exclusive patents, strong brands, or economies of scale, are better positioned to grow rapidly.

Example Analysis: The fictional company "GHI Corp." exhibits a revenue growth of 30% per year and a profit growth of 25% per year. The company possesses cutting-edge technology in the renewable energy sector and holds exclusive patents that give it market leadership.

2. Evaluating Growth Potential

Evaluating a company's growth potential involves a detailed analysis of the market in which it operates and the competence of its management team.

Market Analysis

Market analysis is essential to understand the size and growth potential of the market in which the company operates. This includes:

- **Market Size:** Evaluating the current market size helps understand the scale of opportunities available to the company.

- **Market Growth Potential:** Growing markets offer more opportunities for growth companies. Market growth rates of 20% per year or more indicate a favorable environment for growth companies.

Management Analysis

The competence and vision of the management team are crucial for the success of a growth company. This includes:

- **Track Record of Success:** A management team with a proven track record of driving growth is a good indicator that the company can continue growing.

- **Strategic Vision:** The management team's ability to identify and capitalize on market opportunities is essential for sustaining long-term growth.

Example Analysis: The company "GHI Corp." operates in a renewable energy market valued at $10 billion, with a growth potential of 20% per year. The management team has a proven track record of innovation and success in the sector.

3. Risk Acceptance

Growth investing involves accepting higher volatility and risk in exchange for the potential for high returns.

This requires a tolerance for risk and a willingness to face uncertainty.

Risk Tolerance

Growth investors must be prepared to face stock price volatility and the possibility that projected growth may not materialize. This includes:

- **Price Volatility:** Stocks of growth companies tend to be more volatile due to uncertainty about future growth.

- **Execution Risk:** The risk that the company may not be able to execute its growth strategy as planned.

Advantages and Disadvantages of Growth Investing

Advantages

- **Potential for High Returns:** Growth companies can provide significant returns as they increase their revenues and profits.

- **Opportunity to Invest in Innovative and Disruptive Companies:** Growth investors have the chance to invest in companies that are changing the dynamics of their sectors and creating new markets.

Disadvantages

- **Higher Risk and Volatility:** Uncertainty about future growth can lead to higher volatility in stock prices and the possibility of significant losses.

- **Possibility of Paying an Excessive Premium:** Investors may end up paying an excessive price for growth stocks, especially if growth expectations are not met.

Case Study: Fictional Company "GHI Corp."

Let's consider the fictional company "GHI Corp." to illustrate the application of growth investing.

Growth Rates

- **Revenue Growth:** 30% per year
- **Profit Growth:** 25% per year

Innovation and Competitive Advantage

- **Innovative Product:** Cutting-edge technology in the renewable energy sector
- **Competitive Advantage:** Exclusive patents and market leadership

Evaluating Growth Potential

- **Market Size:** $10 billion
- **Market Growth Potential:** 20% per year

Dividend Investing

Dividend investing is a strategy that involves buying stocks of companies that pay regular and growing dividends. This approach is popular among investors seeking to generate a stable and growing passive income, in addition to benefiting from potential capital appreciation. Below, we explore the key components of dividend investing in greater depth.

1. Identifying Dividend-Paying Companies

Identifying companies that consistently pay dividends is the first crucial step in this strategy. This involves analyzing various factors that indicate the company's ability and willingness to pay dividends.

Dividend Payment History

Companies with a consistent history of paying dividends are generally more stable and reliable. A history of dividend payments over several years, especially during difficult economic periods, is a good indicator of the company's financial strength.

Example: Companies like "JKL Corp." that have a consistent dividend payment history over the past 10 years are considered good candidates for dividend investors.

Dividend Growth Rate

The dividend growth rate is an important indicator of the company's ability to increase payments to shareholders over time. Companies that regularly increase their dividends demonstrate a commitment to profit distribution and sound financial management.

Example: "JKL Corp." has a dividend growth rate of 5% per year, indicating a positive trend of increasing income for investors.

2. Evaluating Dividend Sustainability

Evaluating the sustainability of dividends is essential to ensure that the company can continue to pay and increase dividends in the future. This involves analyzing various financial indicators.

Payout Ratio

The payout ratio is the proportion of profits that the company pays out as dividends. A healthy payout ratio is generally below 70%, indicating that the company retains a significant portion of profits to reinvest in its operations and sustain future growth.

Example: "JKL Corp." has a payout ratio of 60%, which is considered healthy and sustainable.

Free Cash Flow

Free cash flow is the amount of cash that the company generates after covering all its operating and capital expenses. A robust free cash flow is crucial for sustaining dividend payments, especially during periods of volatile profits.

Example: "JKL Corp." generates a free cash flow of $500,000, indicating a strong capacity to sustain and increase dividends.

3. Income Diversification

Diversifying the source of dividend income is an important strategy to reduce risk and increase the stability of passive income.

Sector Diversification

Investing in companies from different sectors helps mitigate the risk associated with any specific sector. Sectors like energy, consumer goods, and healthcare are known for housing companies that consistently pay dividends.

Example: "JKL Corp." operates in diversified sectors such as energy, consumer goods, and healthcare, providing a solid and diversified base of dividend income.

Advantages and Disadvantages of Dividend Investing

Advantages

- **Stable and Growing Passive Income:** Dividend investors can rely on a regular source of passive income, which can grow over time as companies increase their dividends.

- **Lower Volatility:** Stocks of companies that pay dividends tend to be less volatile compared to growth stocks, providing greater portfolio stability.

Disadvantages

- **Lower Potential for Capital Growth:** Companies that regularly pay dividends may reinvest less in their operations, resulting in lower potential for capital growth compared to growth companies.

- **Risk of Dividend Cuts:** During financial difficulties, companies may reduce or eliminate dividend payments, negatively impacting investors' income.

Case Study: Fictional Company "JKL Corp."

Let's consider the fictional company "JKL Corp." to illustrate the application of dividend investing.

Dividend Payment History

- **Dividend Payments:** Consistent over the past 10 years
- **Dividend Growth:** 5% per year

Evaluating Dividend Sustainability

- **Payout Ratio:** 60%
- **Free Cash Flow:** $500,000

Income Diversification

- **Sectors:** Energy, Consumer Goods, Healthcare

Advanced Strategies in Dividend Investing

For investors who wish to delve deeper into dividend investing, there are several advanced strategies to consider.

Dividend Aristocrats

Dividend Aristocrats are companies that not only pay dividends regularly but also increase their dividends annually for at least 25 consecutive years. Investing in Dividend Aristocrats can provide greater security and income predictability.

Example: Companies like "JKL Corp." that have a history of dividend growth can be considered Dividend Aristocrats if they continue to increase their dividends annually.

Dividend Reinvestment

Dividend reinvestment involves using the dividends received to buy more shares of the same company. This can accelerate portfolio growth and increase dividend income over time.

Example: An investor in "JKL Corp." may choose to reinvest the dividends received to buy more shares of the company, thereby increasing their stake and future dividend income.

Evaluating Dividend Yield

The dividend yield is the ratio of the annual dividend paid per share to the stock price. A high dividend yield can indicate a good income opportunity but can also be a sign of risk if the dividends are not sustainable.

Example: If "JKL Corp." pays an annual dividend of $2.00 per share and the stock price is $40.00, the dividend yield is 5%. This can be attractive for investors seeking significant passive income.

Conclusion

Advanced investing is a journey that requires dedication, continuous study, and a deep understanding of the various techniques and strategies available. Fundamental analysis and technical analysis are essential pillars for evaluating stocks and other assets, each offering a unique and valuable perspective. Fundamental analysis focuses on a company's financial fundamentals, while technical analysis is based on price patterns and trading volumes. When combined, both approaches can provide a more complete and robust market view.

In addition to analysis techniques, investment strategies play a crucial role in building a successful portfolio. Value investing, growth investing, and dividend investing are just some of the approaches investors can adopt to achieve their financial goals. Each strategy has its own advantages and disadvantages, and the right strategy choice depends on the investor's individual goals, risk tolerance, and investment horizon.

Value investing involves seeking undervalued stocks, offering a margin of safety and potential appreciation. Growth investing, on the other hand, focuses on companies with high expansion potential, even if it means paying a premium for these stocks. Dividend investing provides a stable and growing passive income, ideal for those seeking a regular income source.

Applying these techniques and strategies requires not only knowledge but also discipline and patience. The financial market is dynamic and can be influenced by a variety of economic, political, and social factors. Therefore, it is essential for investors to stay informed and updated on market trends and changes.

Moreover, diversification is a fundamental practice for risk management. By spreading investments across different asset classes, sectors, and geographies, investors can reduce volatility and protect their portfolios against significant losses. Diversification does not eliminate risk but can help mitigate its impacts.

Another important aspect is emotional management. The financial market can be volatile and unpredictable, and it is common for investors to face periods of uncertainty and stress. Staying calm, following the investment plan, and avoiding impulsive decisions are essential attitudes for long-term success.

Finally, continuous financial education is vital. The investment world is constantly evolving, with new opportunities and challenges regularly emerging. Participating in courses, reading books, following financial news, and learning from other investors are effective ways to enhance investment knowledge and skills.

This book is designed to provide a solid foundation of knowledge and practical strategies to help you build wealth and achieve financial security. By applying the principles and techniques discussed, you will be better prepared to make informed decisions and achieve your long-term financial goals. Remember that the journey to financial prosperity is a continuous process, and each step you take brings you closer to your goals. Keep learning, adapting, and investing wisely, and you will be on the right path to building a secure and prosperous financial future.

Chapter 9: Retirement Planning

Importance of Retirement Planning

Ensuring a comfortable retirement is one of the most important and challenging financial goals a person can have. Retirement marks a phase of life where income from work generally ceases, and it becomes necessary to rely on savings and investments accumulated over the years. Therefore, proper planning is crucial to ensure that you can maintain your standard of living and enjoy a peaceful and secure retirement.

Starting to Plan Early

One of the fundamental principles of retirement planning is to start early. The earlier you begin saving and investing for retirement, the more time your money has to grow. This is due to the power of compound interest, where the gains on your investments generate even more gains over time. For example, if you start investing $500 per month at age 25, with an annual return rate of 7%, you will have accumulated approximately $1.2 million by age 65. However, if you start the same monthly contribution at age 35, you will have accumulated only about $600,000 by age 65. The difference is significant and illustrates the importance of starting early.

Factors Impacting Retirement Planning

1. **Inflation:** Inflation is a critical factor to consider in retirement planning. Inflation reduces the purchasing power of money over time, meaning you will need more money in the future to maintain the same standard of living. For example, if the average inflation rate is 3% per year, something that costs $1,000 today will cost about $2,427 in 30 years. Therefore, it is essential that your investments outpace inflation to ensure you can maintain your purchasing power in retirement.

2. **Life Expectancy:** Life expectancy is increasing, meaning people are living longer in retirement. This is positive, but it also means you will need more resources to sustain a longer retirement period. Planning to live until age 90 or beyond is a prudent practice, ensuring that you do not

exhaust your financial resources before the end of your life.

3. **Lifestyle:** Your desired lifestyle in retirement also impacts how much you will need to save. If you plan to travel frequently, buy a vacation home, or engage in expensive activities, you will need a larger retirement fund. It is important to clearly define your goals and expectations for retirement to accurately calculate how much you will need to save.

Examples of Successful Retirement Plans

1. **Traditional Retirement Plan:** Consider the example of John, who started saving for retirement at age 30. He regularly contributed to a private retirement plan and invested in a diversified portfolio of stocks and bonds. John also adjusted his contributions over the years to keep up with inflation. By age 65, he had accumulated a substantial retirement fund that allows him to live comfortably, travel, and enjoy his hobbies without financial worries.

2. **FIRE (Financial Independence, Retire Early) Plan:** Maria adopted the FIRE philosophy, which involves saving and investing aggressively to achieve financial independence and retire early. She started saving 50% of her income at age 25 and invested in low-cost index funds. By age 45, Maria achieved her goal of financial independence and retired, living off her investments and dedicating her time to personal projects and volunteering.

Planning Tools

To build a robust retirement plan, it is essential to use a combination of planning tools and long-term investments. Below, we present some of the main tools and how they can be used to ensure a comfortable retirement.

Retirement Plans

1. **Social Security:** Social Security is a basic source of income for many retirees. In the United States, the Social Security Administration (SSA) provides retirement benefits for workers who

contribute to the system. While Social Security provides a foundation of income, it is generally not enough to cover all retirement expenses. Therefore, it is important to supplement Social Security with other forms of savings and investment.

2. **Private Retirement Plans:** Private retirement plans are valuable tools for supplementing Social Security. There are two main types of private retirement plans in the United States: 401(k) plans and Individual Retirement Accounts (IRAs). A 401(k) is typically offered by employers and allows employees to contribute pre-tax income, which grows tax-deferred until withdrawal. IRAs, on the other hand, can be opened independently and offer tax advantages depending on the type (Traditional or Roth). Both plans allow you to accumulate resources over time and offer options for lifetime or fixed-term income in retirement.

Long-Term Investments

1. **Stocks:** Investing in stocks can provide significant capital growth over time. Stocks represent partial ownership in a company and offer potential for appreciation and dividends. However, stocks are also volatile and can present risks. It is important to diversify your stock holdings and consider a long-term approach to mitigate risks.

2. **Bonds:** Bonds are fixed-income investments that offer regular interest payments and return of principal at maturity. They are generally considered less risky than stocks and can provide stability to your retirement portfolio. Government bonds, such as U.S. Treasuries, are particularly safe, while corporate bonds may offer higher yields but with greater risk.

3. **Mutual Funds:** Mutual funds allow you to invest in a diversified portfolio of assets managed by professionals. There are various types of funds, including stock funds, bond funds, real estate funds, and multi-asset funds. Index funds and

ETFs, as discussed earlier, are low-cost options that offer instant diversification.

4. **Real Estate:** Investing in real estate can be an effective way to generate passive income and diversify your retirement portfolio. Rental properties can provide a steady income stream, while property appreciation can increase your wealth over time. However, investing in real estate also requires considerations about maintenance, tenant management, and market volatility.

Other Retirement Planning Tools

1. **Retirement Savings Accounts:** Retirement savings accounts, such as the 401(k) and IRAs in the United States, offer a secure way to accumulate resources for retirement. While these accounts have relatively low yields, they offer security and liquidity.

2. **Life and Disability Insurance:** Life and disability insurance can provide financial protection for your family in case of death or disability. They ensure that your loved ones are

financially protected and can complement your retirement plan.

3. **Tax Planning:** Tax planning is an important part of retirement planning. Maximizing tax benefits, such as deductions and exemptions, can significantly increase the value of your retirement savings. Consulting a financial planner or accountant can help identify tax planning opportunities.

Comparisons and Evaluations

To help readers choose the best retirement planning options, it is useful to compare and evaluate the different tools available. Below, we present a comparative table of the main retirement planning tools:

PLANNING TOOL	ADVANTAGES	DISADVANTAGES	SUITABLE FOR
Social Security	Guaranteed income, security	Limited benefits, may not cover all expenses	All workers

PLANNING TOOL	ADVANTAGES	DISADVANTAGES	SUITABLE FOR
Private Retirement Plans (401(k)/IRA)	Tax benefits, supplemental income	Management fees, complexity	Those who want to supplement Social Security
Stocks	Growth potential, dividends	Volatility, risk	Long-term investors with risk tolerance
Bonds	Stability, interest payments	Lower yields, inflation risk	Conservative investors
Mutual Funds	Diversification, professional management	Management fees, market risk	Investors seeking diversification

PLANNING TOOL	ADVANTAGES	DISADVANTAGES	SUITABLE FOR
Real Estate	Passive income, appreciation	Maintenance, tenant management	Investors wanting to diversify with tangible assets
Retirement Savings Accounts (401(k)/IRA)	Security, liquidity	Low yields	Formal workers
Life and Disability Insurance	Financial protection, security	Premiums, complexity	Those who want to protect their family financially
Tax Planning	Maximization of tax benefits	Complexity, need for consultancy	All investors

Conclusion

Planning for retirement is an ongoing process that requires attention, discipline, and a strategic approach. Starting early, considering factors such as inflation and life expectancy, and using a combination of planning tools are essential steps to ensure a comfortable retirement. By following the guidelines and strategies presented in this chapter, you will be better prepared to build a robust retirement plan and achieve your long-term financial goals. Remember to review and adjust your plan regularly to adapt to changes in personal circumstances and the financial market. With careful planning and a proactive approach, you can ensure a secure and prosperous retirement.

Chapter 10: Financial Education for Families

Teaching Finances to Children

Financial education is an essential skill that should be cultivated from an early age. Teaching children about money, saving, and investing not only prepares them for a healthy financial future but also helps develop a responsible and conscious mindset regarding consumption and the value of work. Below, we will explore the importance of financial education for young people and provide practical tips, activities, and educational resources to facilitate this learning.

Importance of Early Financial Education

Introducing financial concepts to children is crucial for several reasons:

1. **Formation of Healthy Habits:** Children who learn about finances early tend to develop healthy financial habits that last a lifetime. They learn to value money, understand the

importance of saving, and distinguish between needs and wants.

2. **Informed Decision-Making:** Financial education empowers children to make informed decisions about money. They learn to evaluate options, consider consequences, and make choices that benefit their long-term financial well-being.

3. **Prevention of Financial Problems:** By understanding basic financial concepts, children are less likely to fall into financial traps, such as excessive debt and impulsive spending, when they become adults.

4. **Development of Planning Skills:** Financial education teaches children to plan and set financial goals. They learn the importance of setting objectives, creating budgets, and tracking their progress.

Practical Tips for Teaching Children About Money

1. **Use Everyday Examples:** Take advantage of daily situations to teach financial lessons. For example, while shopping, explain the difference between prices and values, and how to compare products to find the best value for money.

2. **Give Allowance:** Providing a regular allowance to children is an excellent way to teach money management. Set clear rules on how the allowance should be used, encouraging saving, responsible spending, and donating.

3. **Create a Savings System:** Help children create a savings system, such as a piggy bank or a savings account. Explain the importance of saving for future goals and encourage them to set savings targets.

4. **Teach About Work and Reward:** Teach children that money is earned through work. Give them household chores or small paid jobs so they understand the relationship between effort and reward.

5. **Use Educational Games and Activities:** Board games, apps, and educational

activities can make financial learning fun and engaging. Games like "Monopoly" and "Cashflow" are great for teaching financial concepts in a playful way.

Activities and Educational Resources

1. **Board Games:** Games like "Monopoly" and "Cashflow" are excellent tools for teaching children about finances. They help understand concepts like investment, cash flow, and the importance of making strategic financial decisions.

2. **Educational Apps:** There are several educational apps that teach children about finances interactively. Examples include "PiggyBot," "Bankaroo," and "iAllowance."

3. **Children's Books on Finances:** Books like "The Money Savvy Pig" by Susan Beacham and "Rich Dad Poor Dad for Teens" by Robert Kiyosaki are great resources for introducing financial concepts in an accessible and interesting way.

4. **Practical Activities:** Involve children in practical activities, such as creating a budget for a birthday party, planning a trip, or managing a small garage sale. These activities help apply financial concepts in real situations.

5. **Family Discussions:** Hold regular family meetings to discuss finances. Involve children in conversations about budgeting, saving, and the family's financial goals. This helps normalize the dialogue about money and promote a culture of financial transparency.

Family Financial Planning

Effectively managing family finances is essential to ensure financial stability and achieve long-term goals. A well-structured family financial plan involves creating a budget, setting financial goals, and involving all family members in the process. Below, we discuss the importance of a family budget and provide examples of strategies and tools to help families achieve their financial goals.

Importance of a Family Budget

1. **Expense Control:** A family budget helps monitor and control expenses. It allows the family to see where the money is going and identify areas where savings can be made.

2. **Goal Planning:** A budget facilitates planning and setting financial goals. It helps the family prioritize and allocate resources to achieve specific objectives, such as buying a house, paying for children's education, or planning a trip.

3. **Debt Prevention:** By tracking income and expenses, a budget helps avoid unnecessary debt. It allows the family to live within its means and avoid overspending.

4. **Emergency Preparation:** A well-planned budget includes creating an emergency fund. This ensures that the family is prepared to handle financial surprises, such as medical expenses or unexpected repairs.

Strategies for Managing Family Finances

1. **Creating a Family Budget:** Start by listing all sources of family income, such as salaries, investment returns, and other money inflows. Then, list all expenses, including housing, food, transportation, education, leisure, and other recurring expenses. Subtract expenses from income to determine the available balance.

2. **Setting Financial Goals:** Establish short, medium, and long-term financial goals. Short-term goals may include creating an emergency fund or paying off debts. Medium-term goals may involve buying a car or renovating the house. Long-term goals may include buying a house or retirement.

3. **Involving All Family Members:** Involve all family members in financial planning. Hold regular family meetings to discuss the budget, financial goals, and progress made. This promotes shared responsibility and collaboration.

4. **Using Financial Management Tools:** Use financial management tools, such as budget

spreadsheets, personal finance apps, and accounting software. These tools help track income and expenses, monitor financial goals, and identify areas for improvement.

5. **Creating an Emergency Fund:** Establish an emergency fund to cover unexpected expenses. Ideally, the emergency fund should cover three to six months of basic expenses. Keep this fund in a separate and accessible account.

6. **Continuous Financial Education:** Promote continuous financial education for all family members. Encourage reading books on finance, attending courses and workshops, and seeking updated information on investments and financial planning.

Examples of Tools and Resources for Family Financial Planning

1. **Budget Spreadsheets:** Use budget spreadsheets to record income and expenses. There are several spreadsheets available online that can be customized to the family's needs.

2. **Personal Finance Apps:** Apps like "YNAB" (You Need A Budget), "Mint," and "PocketGuard" are excellent for tracking the budget, monitoring expenses, and setting financial goals.

3. **Accounting Software:** Software like "Quicken" and "QuickBooks" offer advanced financial management features, including detailed reports, charts, and analyses.

4. **Books on Family Finances:** Books like "Rich Dad Poor Dad" by Robert Kiyosaki, "Secrets of the Millionaire Mind" by T. Harv Eker, and "The Richest Man in Babylon" by George S. Clason are great resources for learning about personal finance and financial planning.

5. **Courses and Workshops:** Attend courses and workshops on personal finance and investments. Many financial institutions and organizations offer free or affordable educational programs.

Examples of Family Financial Planning Strategies

1. **50/30/20 Method:** This budgeting method divides net income into three categories: 50% for needs (housing, food, transportation), 30% for wants (leisure, entertainment), and 20% for savings and debt repayment. This approach helps balance expenses and ensure that a significant portion of income is allocated to savings.

2. **Zero-Based Budgeting:** In zero-based budgeting, every dollar of income is assigned to a specific category, so that the sum of expenses and savings equals the total income. This ensures that every dollar has a purpose and helps avoid unnecessary spending.

3. **Cash Envelope System:** The cash envelope system involves distributing income into different envelopes, each designated for a specific expense category. When the money in an envelope runs out, no more can be spent in that category until the next budget period. This method is effective for controlling spending and avoiding debt.

4. **Automating Savings:** Set up automatic transfers to savings and investment accounts. Automating savings ensures that a portion of income is allocated to financial goals before it can be spent.

5. **Regular Budget Review:** Regularly review the budget to adjust expense categories and ensure that financial goals are being met. Periodic review helps identify areas where savings can be made and make adjustments as needed.

Conclusion

Financial education for families is an essential component for ensuring long-term financial stability and well-being. Teaching children about money, saving, and investing from an early age prepares them for a healthy and responsible financial future. Additionally, a well-structured family financial plan, involving creating a budget, setting financial goals, and involving all family members, is crucial for achieving financial goals and avoiding financial problems.

By using practical strategies, financial management tools, and educational resources, families can develop healthy financial habits, make informed decisions, and be prepared to face unexpected events. Continuous financial education and collaboration among family members are essential for building a solid financial foundation and ensuring a prosperous and secure future for all.

Final Chapter: The Beginning of the Practical Journey

The Start of Consolidation

You might find it a bit strange to reach the end of this book and encounter the title of this chapter: "The Beginning." Why beginning? The reason is quite simple. This is the beginning of the practical part, the start of the reality you will create with the knowledge you have gained throughout this reading. It is the beginning of consolidation. After all, all the information acquired throughout the chapters becomes a part of you. It becomes part of your intellectual advancements, especially because knowledge is one of the few things that cannot be taken away from a human being. Possessions, time, people can be taken, but knowledge cannot be expelled from the mind once it has entered.

All the data shared throughout this book resulted from extensive studies in the field, practical executions, but above all, stem from a foundation that has shaped a mindset over many years. Years of studying philosophies like Stoicism, which advocates a realistic view of reality, enjoying the present while acknowledging that many things are within our control and that, even coexisting with many of them, it is possible (and necessary) to seek the greater good: freedom. It is a purpose of living today while preparing for tomorrow, recognizing the possibilities of adversities arising, and seeking to be prepared to deal with them without preventing the achievement of personal fulfillment in its many nuances.

Thus, you may wonder why such philosophical issues are addressed in a book where numbers, terms, and charts have guided us. The reason is simple. All the money sought is not an end in itself. It is the means to achieve freedom. Money is the icon that, in our society, allows us to achieve the freedom to have or not have, to do or not do, to go or not go, to say yes or no. Therefore, we always prioritize the pursuit of cautious actions, such as creating reserves or setting deadlines to find the right moment to stop, and the idealization of goals and dreams we wish to achieve.

A passage from Epictetus' Manual (one of the most famous Stoics in history) says the following:

"Of things that exist, some are within our control, others are not. Within our control are judgment, desire, aversion – in short, everything that is our own action. Not within our control are the body, possessions, reputation, public offices. In short – everything that is not our own action." (Epictetus, 125 AD, p.15)

In this fragment, the Stoic outlines everything we can control with our actions. We can only care about what is within our options to act. Society, political reality, people's opinions, events around us – all these things are not subject to our command. However, there are many where we have the power of decision. Where we can judge, evaluate, choose what we believe is worth it or not. Including, where we should work, for how much, where we can invest, what things we should study, what risks we are willing to take, and what we are not willing to sacrifice. This same Greek philosopher, in one of his musings, states that all those who try to control the world will fail. Therefore, accepting this truth is essential to living carefully, balancing prudence and boldness, being ready to deal with adversities.

Much has been said throughout this book about the importance of money. But it is essential to know that it is much more valuable to be free than to be rich. Because if money enslaves you, it will not be useful to you. If it absolutely robs you of energy, time, and pleasures, then no amount will be enough, and it will be your prison. Money cannot be greater than what you deem essential. It must exist to provide you with freedom.

Be practical with money. Do not let it dominate you; you must command it. Always keep in mind what money can do for you and its most fundamental purposes. Know when to stop and live off your income. Do not be the richest man in the cemetery. Accumulate your capital, but plan to enjoy it in life and in time to make the most of it. Adjust your earnings to achieve your goals, calculate based on your reality, but be coherent with your efforts. This means you should indeed project with audacity, but you cannot go in circles.

A classic example is the story of a businessman and a fisherman. The fisherman, who lived peacefully in his village, caught only two fish a day, one to eat and the other to sell, as he needed money to buy spices and other complementary foods to the daily fish. The businessman, bothered by the fisherman's 'lack of vision,' asked him why he did not catch as many fish as he could daily for a while. According to the businessman, this way, he could hire more people to fish with him, open his own business, generate more profits, and accumulate wealth. Wealth that, according to the businessman, would serve so that the fisherman would not have to worry about anything else, besides being able to do what he likes and have what he needs to live. The fisherman said he did not need to go through all these steps to reach that goal because, even without going through all these stages, he already lived his goal. He did not worry about anything outside his priorities and spent his time doing what he enjoyed, being able to even enjoy this hobby in his needs.

This does not mean we should reduce the effort applied in our economic trajectory. However, it is important to know where you want to go, what you want to achieve, and, of course, everything you already have that can help you in your quest for success in achieving freedom.

Discovering Where You Are

As clarified throughout this book, all the basic fundamentals regarding investments and financial organization have been duly passed on to you. However, the study part is far from over. Those who deal with the market need to recognize its rapid ability to evolve and change the scenarios (often even radically). Therefore, it is always necessary to study to stay updated and follow the directions the world is generally heading. After all, many things can cause significant impacts in the financial segment, and being always alert is a good strategy to avoid being surprised or financially sinking due to a lack of adaptation.

In this sense, something relevant to do when going into action, that is, opening your portfolio, starting your contributions, and putting your capital (whatever amount it may be) at stake, is a basic necessity to discover WHERE YOU ARE within your projections, goals, deadlines, possibilities. It is essential to verify what your profile is.

This is because each individual is unique, with distinct values and beliefs, which will reflect in an investment portfolio adjusted to that profile. As soon as you identify your own profile, it is recommended that you reflect on the variety of asset distribution in your portfolio. This means you should not place all applications in a single type of asset, as we are already aware that the financial market has instability as a predominant characteristic in its existence, just as we know that to achieve faster and more significant growth, it is important to also invest in modalities that offer more, regardless of the risks.

Conclusion: The Beginning of the Practical Journey

All the modules in this book aimed to convey the necessary knowledge, not only about investments, including the entire range of these in the U.S. and abroad, the ways to execute procedures and transactions, the ways to analyze companies, values, to understand the functioning of the financial market, but also to know yourself, have an idea of your horizon, what your dreams are, what you consider essential to live, what motivates you to strive for more, and why you would sacrifice relevant things to achieve your projects.

In the course "Building Wealth: Practical Strategies for Prosperity and Financial Security," it is possible to have a general overview, not specific as in many cases, but that can help a completely layperson have good knowledge and notions of how they can better use and invest their own earnings. It is, beyond the theoretical and technical part, an attempt to share real-life experience, permeated by stumbles and achievements, and transformed into a mindset that, at worst, will make you stop to reflect, and at best, will transform you as well.

However, this module needs to be concluded by recalling the title that heads it: the beginning. The beginning of practice. The only way that can lead to perfection. And much more than mastering tools and information, it is necessary to master oneself, being aware that not everything can be controlled or predicted.

No course will teach you everything. After all, no one knows everything. No one is exempt from having to study, search, analyze, and continue advancing. This is not an ending. It is the basics for creating an investment portfolio and making it profitable. Here ends everything that, within investments, we consider the truth. Beyond that, we will have the post-truth and subjects even more complex than those finalized in the conclusion of this transition.

Building wealth and financial security are continuous journeys. This book was just the beginning. From here, it is up to you to apply the knowledge acquired, continue learning, and adapt to changes. The journey to financial prosperity is unique for each individual, and I hope this book has been a useful and inspiring guide in your path.

Conclusion

Summary of Key Points

Throughout this book, we explored various practical strategies for building wealth and achieving financial security. Below, we recap the main lessons from each chapter, highlighting the most important points and strategies discussed.

Introduction

- **Book Objective:** We highlighted the importance of building wealth and financial security, providing more freedom, opportunities, and peace of mind.

- **Importance of the Topic:** We discussed how practical strategies are essential for achieving financial prosperity, transforming theory into concrete actions.

Chapter 1: Understanding Wealth

- **Definition of Wealth:** We explored different perspectives on what it means to be rich and prosperous.

- **Benefits of Wealth:** We discussed how wealth can improve the quality of life and provide security.

Chapter 2: Financial Planning

- **Setting Financial Goals:** We covered how to establish short, medium, and long-term financial goals.

- **Budgeting and Expense Control:** We presented techniques for creating and maintaining an effective budget.

Chapter 3: Debt Management

- **Types of Debt:** We differentiate between good and bad debts.

- **Debt Repayment Strategies:** We describe methods such as the snowball and avalanche techniques to eliminate debt.

Chapter 4: Savings and Emergency Fund

- **Importance of Savings:** We explain why having a financial reserve is crucial.

- **Building an Emergency Fund:** We detail how much to save and where to keep this money.

Chapter 5: Introduction to Investments

- **Types of Investments:** We describe different types of investments, such as stocks, bonds, and cryptocurrencies.

- **Risk and Return:** We explain how to evaluate the risk and potential return of different investments.

Chapter 6: Portfolio Diversification

- **Importance of Diversification:** We discuss how diversification can reduce risks.

- **Diversification Strategies:** We provide practical examples of how to diversify an investment portfolio.

Chapter 7: Investments for Beginners

- **First Steps:** We explain how to start investing with little money.

- **Investment Platforms:** We present tools and apps that make investing easier for beginners.

Chapter 8: Advanced Investments

- **Fundamental and Technical Analysis:** We explain methods for evaluating stocks and other assets.

- **Investment Strategies:** We describe different investment strategies, such as value investing and growth investing.

Chapter 9: Retirement Planning

- **Importance of Retirement Planning:** We explain how to ensure a comfortable retirement.

- **Planning Tools:** We present retirement plans and long-term investments.

Chapter 10: Financial Education for Families

- **Teaching Finances to Children:** We explain how to introduce financial concepts to the younger generation.

- **Family Financial Planning:** We describe how to manage family finances effectively.

Next Steps

The journey of building wealth and financial security does not end with reading this book. It is a continuous process that requires constant learning, adaptation to financial changes, and practical action. Below, we provide guidance on how to continue this journey and advance your financial goals.

1. **Keep Learning:** Financial education is an ongoing process. Continue seeking knowledge through books, courses, workshops, and online resources. Stay updated on financial market trends and new investment strategies.

2. **Adapt to Changes:** The financial market is constantly evolving. Be prepared to adapt to economic, political, and technological changes. Regularly review your financial plan and make adjustments as necessary.

3. **Apply Acquired Knowledge:** Put into practice the strategies discussed in this book. Create a budget, set financial goals, eliminate debt, build an emergency fund, and start investing. Practical action is essential to achieving your financial goals.

4. **Diversify Your Investments:** Continue diversifying your investment portfolio to reduce risks and maximize returns. Explore new investment opportunities and adjust your strategy as needed.

5. **Plan for the Long Term:** Keep your focus on long-term goals, such as retirement. Continue contributing to your retirement plans and long-term investments.

6. **Involve Your Family:** Involve all family members in financial planning. Promote continuous financial education and encourage active participation in financial decisions.

7. **Review and Adjust Regularly:** Regularly review your financial plan and make adjustments as necessary. Track your progress toward financial goals and make changes to ensure you are on the right path.

8. **Seek Professional Guidance:** Consider seeking the guidance of a financial advisor to help plan and manage your finances. A

professional can provide valuable insights and help optimize your financial strategy.

9. **Maintain a Positive Mindset:** Building wealth is a journey that requires patience, discipline, and perseverance. Maintain a positive mindset and be prepared to face challenges and learn from mistakes.

10. **Celebrate Your Achievements:** Recognize and celebrate your financial achievements along the way. Each goal achieved is an important step toward financial security and prosperity.

By following these guidelines and applying the knowledge acquired, you will be well-equipped to continue your journey of building wealth and achieving financial security. Remember that financial success is a continuous process and that each step taken toward your goals is a significant achievement. Good luck on your financial journey!

Recommended Reading

To continue your journey of building wealth and financial security, it is essential to deepen your knowledge and explore different perspectives on personal finance, investments, and financial planning. Below, we suggest a selection of books and resources that complement the content of this book and offer valuable insights to enhance your financial skills.

1. **"Rich Dad Poor Dad" by Robert T. Kiyosaki**

    - **Description:** This classic in financial education challenges traditional beliefs about money and investments. Kiyosaki shares the lessons he learned from his "rich dad" and his "poor dad," highlighting the importance of acquiring assets that generate passive income and the difference between assets and liabilities.

    - **How It Complements:** "Rich Dad Poor Dad" complements our book by emphasizing the importance of investing in assets that generate passive income and providing a new perspective on financial education and the mindset needed to achieve financial independence.

2. **"Secrets of the Millionaire Mind" by T. Harv Eker**

    - **Description:** Eker explores the beliefs and habits that differentiate millionaires from ordinary people. He presents 17 wealth files that describe the attitudes and behaviors that can help anyone achieve financial success.

    - **How It Complements:** This book complements our content by addressing the mindset and habits necessary to build wealth. It offers insights on how to change limiting beliefs and adopt an abundance mindset.

3. **"The Richest Man in Babylon" by George S. Clason**

- **Description:** Through parables set in ancient Babylon, Clason teaches timeless financial principles, such as the importance of saving, investing wisely, and living within your means.

- **How It Complements:** "The Richest Man in Babylon" reinforces the concepts of saving and investing discussed in our book, offering practical and easy-to-understand lessons on how to manage money effectively.

4. **"Smart Investments" by Gustavo Cerbasi**

    - **Description:** Cerbasi, one of Brazil's leading personal finance experts, offers a practical and accessible approach for those who want to start investing. He explains different types of investments and how to create a personalized investment strategy.

    - **How It Complements:** This book complements our chapter on investments by providing a detailed view of the

Brazilian investment market and practical strategies for beginners and experienced investors.

5. **"The Millionaire Next Door" by Thomas J. Stanley and William D. Danko**

    - **Description:** Based on a study of American millionaires, this book reveals that most millionaires live modestly and built their wealth through prudent financial habits and intelligent investments.

    - **How It Complements:** "The Millionaire Next Door" complements our content by highlighting the importance of living below your means and investing consistently. It offers real-life examples of how ordinary people achieved financial independence.

6. **"The Psychology of Money" by Morgan Housel**

- **Description:** Housel explores how emotions and behaviors influence our financial decisions. He presents 20 lessons on how to think about money and make smarter financial decisions.

- **How It Complements:** This book complements our content by addressing the psychology behind financial decisions. It offers insights on how to manage emotions and behaviors to improve financial health.

7. **"The Intelligent Investor" by Benjamin Graham**

    - **Description:** Considered the bible of value investing, this classic book by Graham teaches the fundamental principles of intelligent investing, including stock analysis and the importance of the margin of safety.

    - **How It Complements:** "The Intelligent Investor" complements our chapter on advanced investments by providing a solid foundation for fundamental analysis and value investing strategies.

8. **"Me Poupe!" by Nathalia Arcuri**

    - **Description:** Nathalia Arcuri, founder of the largest finance channel on YouTube in Brazil, offers practical and accessible tips for saving money, investing, and achieving financial independence.

    - **How It Complements:** This book complements our content by providing practical tips and real-life examples of how to save and invest in the Brazilian context. It is especially useful for those starting their financial journey.

9. **"The Zurich Axioms" by Max Gunther**

    - **Description:** This book presents 12 axioms that guide investors to make smarter financial decisions and manage risks effectively. Based on the practices of Swiss bankers, it offers a unique approach to investing.

- **How It Complements:** "The Zurich Axioms" complements our content by providing practical principles for risk management and investment decision-making. It offers a different perspective on how to approach the financial market.

10. **"Money: Master the Game" by Tony Robbins**

    - **Description:** Robbins interviews some of the world's greatest investors and shares their strategies for achieving financial independence. He offers a step-by-step plan to build wealth and ensure financial security.

    - **How It Complements:** This book complements our content by providing practical strategies and advice from renowned experts. It offers a comprehensive plan to build wealth and achieve financial security.

Additional Resources

In addition to the recommended books, we suggest exploring the following resources to deepen your financial knowledge:

1. **Online Courses:** Platforms like Coursera, Udemy, and Khan Academy offer courses on personal finance, investments, and financial planning. These courses are taught by experts and can be accessed at any time.

2. **Podcasts:** Podcasts like "Finanças e Investimentos" by Gustavo Cerbasi, "Me Poupe! Podcast" by Nathalia Arcuri, and "Investidor Inteligente" by Thiago Nigro offer valuable insights and updates on the financial market.

3. **Finance Blogs and Websites:** Sites like "Me Poupe!", "Dinheirama," and "Investopedia" offer articles, guides, and tools to help improve your financial skills and make informed decisions.

4. **Personal Finance Apps:** Apps like "YNAB" (You Need A Budget), "Mint," and "Guiabolso"

help manage your budget, monitor expenses, and track the progress of your financial goals.

5. **Online Communities:** Join forums and discussion groups on personal finance and investments, such as Reddit (subreddits like r/personalfinance and r/investing) and Facebook groups. These communities offer support, advice, and the opportunity to learn from others' experiences.

By exploring these books and additional resources, you can deepen your financial knowledge, enhance your skills, and continue your journey of building wealth and financial security. Remember that financial education is a continuous process and that each step taken toward learning and practical application is a valuable investment in your financial future.

Afterword

As we conclude this book, "Building Wealth: Practical Strategies for Prosperity and Financial Security," it is important to reflect on the journey we have taken together. From understanding the fundamental concepts of wealth to applying practical strategies to achieve financial security, each chapter was designed to empower you with the knowledge and tools necessary to transform your financial life.

Building wealth is not a destination but a continuous process of learning, adapting, and growing. Throughout this book, we emphasized the importance of setting clear goals, creating a solid financial plan, strategically managing debt, investing wisely, and planning for the future. These are the cornerstones of a successful and secure financial life.

I hope the lessons and strategies presented here have provided valuable and practical insights that you can apply in your daily life. Remember that the journey to financial prosperity is unique for each individual. What works for one person may not work for another, and it is essential to adapt strategies to your personal circumstances and goals.

Financial education is a continuous process. As you progress on your journey, continue seeking knowledge, learning from your experiences, and adjusting your strategies as needed. Resilience and adaptability are essential qualities for navigating the ever-changing financial world.

I would like to express my deepest gratitude to all the readers who embarked on this journey with me. Your dedication to seeking a better financial life is inspiring. I hope this book has been a source of motivation and guidance, and that you feel more confident and empowered to make informed financial decisions.

Finally, remember to share the knowledge you have acquired. Financial education is a powerful legacy that you can pass on to your children, family, and friends. By doing so, you will be contributing to the creation of a more financially aware and prepared generation.

Thank you for allowing me to be part of your journey. I wish you all the success and prosperity in your future financial endeavors.

With gratitude and best wishes,

Derik Silva

www.ingramcontent.com/pod-product-compliance
Lightning Source LLC
Chambersburg PA
CBHW071916210526
45479CB00002B/444